SMITH WIGGLESWORTH
The Secret of His Power

SMITH WIGGLESWORTH
The Secret of His Power

by
Albert Hibbert

HARRISON HOUSE
Tulsa, Oklahoma

Unless otherwise indicated,
all Scripture quotations are taken from
the *King James Version* of the Bible.

05 04 03 02 01   33 32 31 30 29

Smith Wigglesworth: The Secret of His Power
ISBN 0-89274-211-9
Copyright © 1982, 1993 by Albert Hibbert
45 Saint Mary's Walk
Burham Rochester
Kent
ME1 3SJ
ENGLAND

Published by **Harrison House, Inc.**
P. O. Box 35035
Tulsa, Oklahoma 74153

Contents

1 Smith Wigglesworth—The Man 9

2 Smith Wigglesworth—The Spirit 53

3 Smith Wigglesworth—Life in the Spirit 93

SMITH WIGGLESWORTH
The Secret of His Power

1
Smith Wigglesworth
The Man

It was my privilege to know Smith Wigglesworth, not merely as a passing acquaintance, but personally. I had fellowship with him both in my home and in his. We only get to know a person well and learn to appreciate him when we know him in the home. With many ministers we see an entirely different person in the home from the one we see in the pulpit.

The people who saw Smith Wigglesworth only in the pulpit did not get a true picture of the man; they could never appreciate the tender Christlike person he was. They never, or very rarely, saw the tears of compassion he shed; these were only seen by those closely associated with him.

Oral Roberts has said that he and his fellow evangelists owe Wigglesworth a debt beyond calculation. Wigglesworth was an outstanding apostle of faith who taught and inspired many people. The revival that started through his ministry swept this nation from West to East, from North to South. We are still feeling the impact of it today.

One was never the same after having had personal fellowship with Smith Wigglesworth. That which he deposited within a person's spirit was beyond explanation. One could only understand this by experiencing it himself.

Wigglesworth died in March of 1947 at the age of eighty-seven, but his ministry lives on in the experience of multitudes of people. In retrospect I think that more has been accomplished as a result of his ministry since his death than during his entire lifetime.

Meeting Wigglesworth

Smith Wigglesworth and I first came in contact after I had been miraculously healed.

When I was a boy, my mother and I attended a little mission hall in the city of Wakefield, West Yorkshire, England. We went on a cold, wet Thursday night in February, 1923. My recollections are very clear concerning the events of that evening, even to the hymn the people were singing as we went into the hall.

My mother, though a devout Episcopalian who regularly attended the Church of England, had never known the Savior personally. She came to know Him that night. On returning home from the meeting, she told the family that she was "saved," but they didn't understand. My father was a hard character, who worked in the coal mines (as did my three eldest brothers) and was county champion at billiards and an avid gambler. Yet at the same time he was bell ringer and an officer in the local parish church. My brothers were also involved in the church, singing in the choir.

My father's reaction to my mother's announcement was hostile. He forbade her to go to the mission hall again. But because of the influence of my brothers, Mother and I continued to attend the meetings held there.

As Easter drew near, I took ill. The sickness did not seem serious at first; but later I contracted double pneumonia, which at that time was grave. I went into a deep coma. After examining me, a brain specialist said that I would never regain consciousness. He suggested that perhaps this was for the best; since my brain was so badly damaged, if any hope existed of my regaining consciousness, I could be mentally and physically incapacitated for life.

The little mission Mother and I attended was holding an Easter convention in one of the nearby villages. On Easter Saturday I had been in a coma for a week. The doctor said my condition was deteriorating rapidly and that, in his opinion, I could not live through the day. Father went to the convention to ask for prayer at Mother's request.

The pastor, Mr. Richardson, who was a dear friend of Smith Wigglesworth, and Charles Buckley, one of the preachers for the convention, accompanied Mother home. As they arrived, the doctor was leaving. In response to Mr. Richardson's inquiry, the doctor said it was impossible for me to live for more than an hour or, at the most, two. The family gathered together in the sick room; all of them, except Mother thought it was the end. Even though I was desperately sick, they wanted to see me; being the youngest, I was quite a favorite with the family.

Mr. Richardson and Mr. Buckley entered the sickroom. Mr. Buckley then addressed the family.

"God has shown me that a miracle is going to happen today," he said. "What will be your reaction if God heals this boy?"

My eldest brother, a fine young man, answered, "If God heals him, we will serve Him."

Mr. Buckley responded, "You realize that you are not promising me; you are promising God."

My brother said, "We are aware of that."

"We are going to pray," Mr. Buckley then said. "But the healing may not happen immediately, so don't be disappointed if this is the case. God is going to give us a sign before we leave."

When they prayed, nothing happened-apparently. Afterwards they went downstairs for a cup of tea that my sister had prepared for them. Because they had missed the afternoon service, they were going straight to the evening one.

My brothers had bought me an Easter chocolate hen which was sitting on the dressing table. I remember coming out of the coma and shouting, "Mum, where's my chocolate hen?"

I was healed, perfectly. The family accompanied Mr. Richardson and Mr. Buckley to the service and were saved. My father was the first. So convincing was the miracle that, within a short time, fifty-seven of the family and near relations were saved.

Of course, the Devil would not take such a rebuttal without some attempt to negate the work of God. Within a short time I was stricken with acute appendicitis. The doctor came and said that if my life was to be spared, he was to order immediate surgery.

My mother said, "If God has not healed him within two hours, then I will consent to the surgery." The doctor said he could not grant such a request.

"Very well," Mother replied, "if you are not prepared to grant a stay of two hours, I will take full responsibility for what happens."

The doctor said he would return in two hours. When he did, I was asleep and, again, miraculously healed.

Even though Mr. Wigglesworth lived only twenty miles from our home, we had not yet met him. But not long after this event, we met, and he wanted to know all about my miracle. He rejoiced at what God had done just as much as if he had been instrumental in the healing. From that time on, he and my family were close friends.

A Humble Man

Wigglesworth never claimed any glory for any miracle of healing. Only wanting Christ to be seen, he scorned the acclaim of men. In fact, he said that on one occasion God had spoken to him and said, "Wigglesworth, I am going to burn you up until there is no more Wigglesworth left; then only Jesus will be seen." As far as Wigglesworth was concerned, this had happened; he never wanted to be seen.

I will never forget the last time I had fellowship with him. We were sitting at the table in his home. It was one week before he died.

Looking at me with tears in his eyes, he said, "When are you going to move into a realm that you have not yet touched and get going for God?" He went on, "I am an old man, eighty-seven years of age. I may not look it; I certainly don't feel it. But you cannot argue with the birth certificate, and it tells me I am eighty-seven. So I have to accept it, regardless of how I feel about it.

"Today in my mail I had an invitation to Australia, one to India and Ceylon, and one to America. People have their eyes on me." Then he sobbed as if his heart would break. "Poor Wigglesworth," he wept. "What a failure to think that people have their eyes on me. God will never give His glory to another; He will take them from the scene."

I thought, *My God, if this man is a failure, what am I?*

Wigglesworth's Death

Two days later my pastor, Mr. Richardson went home to be with the Lord. His funeral service was to be held exactly one week after my first visit to Wigglesworth's home.

Three of my brothers and I were asked to be pall-bearers at the funeral. We sat on a side seat at the front of the church which was filled to capacity. When Mr. Wigglesworth entered, all eyes turned to look at this erect figure as he walked down the aisle to sit next to the front row.

My father, who had come to the vestry to share the pulpit with those taking part in the service, was joined there by Mr. Wigglesworth. He watched as the sprightly figure left is seat and ascended the steps into the vestry, more like a man of sixty than eighty-seven.

When inside the vestry, Wigglesworth kissed my father and inquired about my sister who was ill. As my father was replying, Wigglesworth stumbled forward suddenly. My father put out an arm to steady him, then gently lowered him to the floor. But Wigglesworth was gone.

James Salter, who was conducting the service, walked out of the vestry and announced to the people, "I have to announce that my father-in-law, Smith Wigglesworth, has just passed away." That was March 12, 1947.

The congregation was shattered. Only a moment before they had seen him go into the vestry. He had no sickness, no pain; he just went home.

A doctor whom I knew well was called to the church. Upon examining the body, he said, "What a fine specimen of manhood! There is no visible cause of death. It is just like a workman coming home from his work, taking off his coat, and settling down to rest."

I thought he described it well.

According to law, the doctor should have performed an autopsy to determine the cause of death before an authorization for burial could be issued. But this was not done. The law of the realm was passed by, even though the proper procedure was clearly laid down! This is the only case in which I have known this to happen. Then I remembered a statement Wigglesworth had made to his wife: "No knife will ever touch this body, in life or in death."

When he was in business as a plumber in Bradford, England, he was taken ill with acute appendicitis. His wife had called the doctor, who told Wigglesworth that he needed immediate surgery. When Wigglesworth said no, the doctor left to go on his rounds; but he became so troubled that he returned to check on Wigglesworth. When Mrs. Wigglesworth told him that her husband had set out on business, the doctor responded, "Well, they will bring him back a corpse then." But they didn't. God healed him.

Wigglesworth had the power to decide that no knife would touch his body in life, but surely death is another matter. How could he have decided that? I could only conclude that he prophesied by faith. It certainly came to pass just as he had said.

But having made the prophecy, he was tested on it. Such a prophecy will certainly be tested. After entering full-time service for God, Wigglesworth suffered acutely with kidney stones. With his underclothing stained with blood, he continued ministering to the sick who were healed. He told the Lord, "You might as well heal me, because I am not going to have an operation." And he never did. In time, he passed every one of those stones, some of them quite miraculously.

As I stood with others at Wigglesworth's graveside, an evangelist working for the Home Mission Bureau said to me, "Albert, what are we going to do now?'' His voice was filled with pathos. All his hopes were being interred with this man of God.

''I'm going on,'' I answered. ''What about you?''

God does not want us to imitate Smith Wigglesworth. There was only one. He was in many ways unique. But God wants us to be ourselves, to catch a glimpse of what we might be in God, because in many cases there is a vast difference between what we are and what we could be in God. We can be as effective in our sphere of labor as Wigglesworth was in his—if we are prepared to pay the price.

Rough Outside—Warm Inside

Wigglesworth was sensitive to the moving of God's Spirit. But because as a man he was outwardly rough, some of his actions or words seemed harsh. I remember an aunt of mine who went to him for prayer concerning a stomach complaint. He punched her in the stomach. She screamed out, but was healed. I have never known anyone to suffer ill effects from such seemingly harsh treatment. Rather, I have known the reverse: The people subjected to such treatment were healed. A person ministering in this manner has to know God; otherwise, such actions could be disastrous.

I remember a reply Wigglesworth once made when questioned as to why he sometimes hit people.

He said, "I don't hit people. I hit the Devil. If they get in the way, I can't help it." He was convinced that all sickness was of the Devil. He used to say, "You can't deal gently with the Devil, nor comfort him; he likes comfort."

Many theologians would disagree with him but, having disagreed, could not produce the tangible evidence in support of their theories that he produced in his ministry. Wigglesworth dealt with the Devil as a reality and took authority over him. This particular action was his way of expressing such authority. To me it was a clear case of the end justifying the means.

We hear so much about acting in faith. What exactly do we mean by that? I ask this because I have seen people genuinely trying to act on what they thought to be faith (and in some cases, what they had been told was faith), but with embarrassing results, which certainly did not glorify God.

If we are to act in faith as Wigglesworth did, then we must live as Wigglesworth lived. Trying to act in faith without living a corresponding life of faith is sheer presumption. I have seen this happen many times. Wigglesworth always maintained that the child of God was in a position of power to deal with the Devil through the blood of Christ—providing that child of God was living right. He was absolutely sold out to the principle of holiness.

Wigglesworth was very forthright in ministry. He never apologized for what he said. An example occurred in a particular meeting of his that I attended. A lady, who at other times had given an utterance in tongues which Wigglesworth had interpreted, began to speak in tongues. Knowing that the woman was not following the Spirit's leading on this occasion, Wigglesworth said gruffly, "Sit down, woman; that is of the flesh."

Wigglesworth was a man who loved the truth. I refer to more than the truth found in the Bible or in a written code; I refer to Wigglesworth's actions, to his personal adherence to scriptural principles. He never exaggerated on any issue. In the field of evangelism, one is sometimes keenly aware that reported numbers of converts and healings are exaggerated. Wigglesworth always reported the details of his meetings exactly as they were, with no embellishments.

Everything he said was 100% true. Any promise he made, he fulfilled without fail. If he had the slightest doubt of being able to fulfill a promise, he preferred not to make it.

At meetings others could easily see that Wigglesworth flowed in the Spirit. Easter time was a special occasion at Preston, England. The Great Convention held at that time was renowned throughout the country. Although he traveled widely, Wigglesworth always tried to be in Preston for this convention, and was usually the one who convened the services. Those who preached at the convention testified of the tremendous liberty they enjoyed there because the presiding preachers did not struggle to create a controlled atmosphere. Whenever Wigglesworth stood up, a tide of blessing rose, because he sought not to draw attention to himself, nor to the preacher, but to Christ.

The Christian Church has failed to make as much of an impact upon the world as it should because of man-centered endeavors. Smith Wigglesworth scorned this very thing, and was open in his condemnation of it. He fully subscribed to Colossians 1:17-19:

> *And he (Jesus) is before all things, and by him all things consist.*
>
> *And he is the head of the body, the church: who is the beginning, the first-born from the dead; that in all things he might have the pre-eminence.*
>
> *For it pleased the Father that in him should all fulness dwell.*

Behind Wigglesworth's rough exterior was an extraordinary compassion. As he read the thousands of letters he received requesting prayer, tears would stream down his face. At such times he was keenly aware of the ravages of sin, which he considered abhorrent.

This awareness of the ravages of sin was one of the secrets of his powerful ministry.

The question has often arisen as to why Jesus wept at Lazarus' tomb when He knew that the rotting corpse was going to respond to words of resurrection life. If He knew that Lazarus was going to rise again, why did he weep? Very simply, He was aware of the ravages of sin, and of how those poor bystanders at the tomb were victims of the devastating power of sin. Why did Jesus say to the women who wept as He went to Calvary, *Weep not for me, but weep for yourselves, and for your children?* (Luke 23:28.) He was aware of what sin had done and of what it was doing. Smith Wigglesworth often wept when faced with the needs of the people because, like Jesus, he was aware of the ravages of sin.

A Simple Man

Wigglesworth could have been a wealthy man. But he counted nothing that he had as being his own. He considered that he himself and all that he had belonged to the Lord. He could have lived in a palace, but instead he chose to be content in a little stone house in Bradford, Yorkshire, England. That home had the atmosphere of God's throne room. The very presence of God could be felt within. I always found it a delight to visit him. It was like going into the sanctuary, into the Cloud of Glory.

Not only did he reach and bless people all over the world through his own ministry, but he also gave liberally to overseas missions. He gave the personal gifts he received, legitimately his, to the work of God, particularly to the Congo Evangelistic Mission, a work very dear to his heart. His daughter Alice and son-in-law James Salter were missionaries on that field. In fact, Salter and W. F. P. Burton were cofounders of the Mission, which today numbers 4,000 churches.

Wigglesworth was very practical. I remember one occasion when I was about to leave his home after visiting on a cold, wet evening. He put his hands upon me in blessing, then counseled, ''Keep that coat well buttoned, and get that collar up. Look after that body. It does not belong to you; it belongs to the Lord. And you will be answerable for it at the Judgment.''

Wigglesworth absolutely opposed the thinking of those who expected their Lord to heal them after doing as they liked with their bodies. He had no sympathy for those who were sick as a result of their own folly.

Feeling that an untidy appearance did not glorify God, Wigglesworth always dressed well. During the days of material depression, people criticized him for this habit. But when he left his plumbing business to engage himself in full-time ministry, he had told the Lord, ''The first time my shoes are down at the heel or my britches need a patch, I shall go back to my business.'' He maintained that if a person trusted God, he would never have to ask for anything because God would look after him.

Wigglesworth proved his point; he never once asked for anything, and he never needed to return to his plumbing business, even though he had a family to support. He always said that God was not stingy but abundant in His provision, enabling one to minister out of that abundance to others. This, Wigglesworth did.

A Holy Man

Smith Wigglesworth believed that a Christian should not be governed by his temperament. Many people are slaves to their anger. Wigglesworth, himself, had at one time been victim of a foul temper. To correct this problem, he got alone with God, shutting himself away until he had complete victory over his emotions. He became the very opposite of what he had been. Instead of violently reacting to circumstances, he was possessed of a great calm, no matter what the circumstance. He never reacted in anger, even in the face of criticism or persecution—and he had his share of both.

Even though he lived in an age when the simplest form of relaxation was considered worldly and evoked condemnation from many Christians,

Wigglesworth was not critical of others. He fully subscribed to John Wesley's definition of worldliness when he wrote in his journal: "Worldliness is that which cools my affection toward God."

Wigglesworth was holy because he had his priorities in the proper order. I once asked him if he ever read a newspaper. He replied, "Beyond a glance at the headlines, no." I then asked him why not. Did he not believe in reading newspapers? He answered that this was not the reason but that he simply did not have the time to read them. Besides, he said, why should he waste the time reading the paper which would give him the partial truth when, by reading the Word of God, he would be assured of getting the whole truth?

"God's Word is preferable to man's word anytime," he used to say.

Wigglesworth believed in total surrender to God. "Very often," he observed, "we try to tame the old man, and we can't do it. But God can, if we are totally surrendered to Him." He set his sights on being like Jesus; hence, his success in the work of the Lord.

Jesus gave us an infallible rule for success. He said, *Follow me, and I will make you fishers of men* (Matt. 4:19). The words *follow me* simply mean "be like me." It was because he did just this that Wigglesworth could accomplish what he did.

Listen to the audacity of the Apostle Paul in his statement to the Christians at Corinth: *Be ye followers of me, even as I also am of Christ* (1 Cor. 11:1). The skeptic would cry, ''Big head! Who does he think he is?'' Yet not one of Paul's critics could produce what he did, in which case, no grounds exist for criticism.

Smith Wigglesworth had no formal education. He was sent to work in the mill at the age of seven. Working twelve to fourteen hours a day, he had no opportunity to go to school. It was not until his twenty-sixth year that Wigglesworth learned to read and write; his wife taught him.

When he and his wife started the Bowland Street Mission in Bradford, his wife was the preacher. Wigglesworth did the menial tasks. But after he was baptized with the Holy Ghost, he was transformed. He preached one night and his wife cried out, ''That's not my Smith!'' The old Smith Wigglesworth was seen no more. Henceforth, for him, to live was Christ.

On New Year's Day, 1913, his beloved wife Mary Jane, whom he affectionately called ''Polly,'' set off to fulfill a preaching engagement. During the trip she died suddenly. The body was taken back to her home. At Brother Wigglesworth's instructions, the lifeless form of his beloved was carried to her room and laid on the bed. When the men who had brought her body had left, Smith closed the door. In the name of Jesus Christ, he rebuked death and ordered it to give her up. His wife opened her eyes and looked straight at him.

"Why have you done this, Smith?" she asked.

"Polly, I need you," he said.

"Smith, my work is finished," she answered. "God wants me."

They talked for quite some time; then Wigglesworth said, "All right, I will let you go."

She lay back upon the pillow and went with the Lord. In such a matter so important to his happiness, Wigglesworth willingly bowed to the will of God.

Smith Wigglesworth had a consuming desire to be like the Savior he loved so well. Once while preaching on Matthew 5:6, he said, "*Hunger and thirst after righteousness* means that nothing else fascinates us so much as being near to God. If there is anything in the heart which savors of condemnation, you cannot pray the prayer of faith. Purity is vital to faith. When you throw your whole heart and life into the plan of God, when you long to be holy, when you long to be pure, then and only then will the law of the Spirit of life make you free from the law of sin and death."

Smith was holy, but he never claimed to be anything other than ordinary. He always claimed that all he had, all he was, was of God.

Not only did Wigglesworth believe in divine healing, but in divine health; and he demonstrated what he believed. His critics have raised this question: "If Wigglesworth believed in divine health, why did he wear glasses for reading?" To be perfectly honest, I don't know. He wore the old-fashioned type which had no supports around the ear, but fit on the nose with a spring. They easily fell off. To keep them from falling to the floor, he wore them on a cord which fastened to his coat. I often saw him put the glasses on to read, then never bother to put them back on after they had fallen from his nose. He left them hanging down and continued to read without them.

At the age of eighty-one he had a full set of natural teeth without a mark of decay. Wanting to expose him as a fraud, a dentist in Switzerland asked Wigglesworth if he might look in his mouth. Smith consented. Afterwards the dentist said he had never seen such a perfect set of teeth.

People have said that one of Wigglesworth's greatest defects was his grammar. It was true that his grammar was not of a high standard; but because he had a mighty anointing, I personally do not think his grammar was an impediment. No impediments exist with the anointing. It makes up for many human failures.

Wigglesworth proved what God could do with a person wholly yielded to Him. An uneducated man with God's anointing accomplishes much more for God than an educated man without it. The blessing of God upon anything will increase its value. In the fourteenth chapter of Matthew, the little lad gave all he had—five loaves and two fishes. But when Jesus took it and blessed it, consider what was accomplished: 5000 men plus women and children were fed!

Smith gave all he had, even in relation to grammar, to his Lord. He once wrote a letter to a university graduate. The next time this person saw Smith, he said, "You know, you spelled the title of the Holy Spirit seven different ways in your letter."

Wigglesworth replied, "Did you understand it?"

"Oh, yes."

Then Wigglesworth said, "Thank God, that's all that matters."

We may be good in the use of English grammar, but what are we doing with that ability? What have we accomplished with our knowledge? Wigglesworth gave what he had to God, and only eternity can reveal what God accomplished through him.

A Man of the Word

Two things dominated Wigglesworth's life and ministry. Firstly, he had a consuming love for the Word of God. Secondly, he had an overwhelming confidence in the God of the Word. What the Word of God said on a subject settled the matter as far as Wigglesworth was concerned. He proved that he was willing to stake his life on what the Bible said when he refused to have an appendectomy.

The following words of the Psalmist fit his experience:

> *O how love I thy law! It is my meditation all the day...*
>
> *I rejoice at thy word, as one that findeth great spoil.*
>
> *I hate and abhor lying: but thy law do I love...*
>
> *Great peace have they which love thy law: and nothing shall offend them.*
>
> *Psalm 119:97, 162, 163, 165*

These four lines of Scripture sum up the character of Smith Wigglesworth.

Wigglesworth never went more than fifteen minutes without reading the Word of God, regardless of where he was or whose company he found himself. During the meals we shared together, eating and speaking of God's Word were interspersed. Wigglesworth would say grace, which was more than a mere sentence, or sometimes, in his cracked voice, he would sing a song of praise. After this, we would have the first course. Then he would read and pray. Following that we would eat the next course. Afterwards, regardless of whether or not it was the last course, he would again read and pray. That was how he lived; his life was not one of monotonous repetition.

One of my brothers became especially aware of Wigglesworth's love for the Word of God on one particular occasion after Wigglesworth had been staying with our family. My brother was taking him to the next place where he was to minister. They had been on the journey for about ten minutes conversing about current events when suddenly Wigglesworth shouted, "Stop!" My brother stopped the vehicle immediately, thinking that something was wrong. But Wigglesworth bowed his head and prayed, "Lord, I am sorry. We have talked about everything but Thee and Thy Word, and the souls of men. Please forgive us." Then turning to my brother, he said, "You can go now." The conversation was changed for the rest of the journey.

Someone once asked Wigglesworth if he could recommend a good book on divine healing. He answered, "Yes, there is only one textbook on that subject: the Word of God."

One of my brothers, on whom Wigglesworth had laid hands, commending him to the ministry of healing, was called to pray for a man who was dying with cancer. The man's life expectancy was only a few weeks.

My brother said to the man, "I am not going to pray for you now, but I will return in a week's time. Meanwhile, I want you to read all the miracles of the New Testament."

My brother returned as he had said and asked the man if he had read the miracles. The man responded that he had read them several times during the week. Immediately, my brother laid hands on the man and he was healed. The Psalmist wrote: *Thou hast magnified thy word above all thy name* (Ps. 138:2).

Smith Wigglesworth had learned the secret of the power of God's Word. He said, "I understand God by His Word. I cannot understand God by impressions or feelings. I cannot get to know God by sentiment. I can only know Him by His Word."

He said, "It is a dangerous practice to be governed by feelings. We are saved not by feelings, but by the Word of God. Salvation does not fluctuate as do feelings."

Most Christians have yet to understand this. They are concerned about fluctuation of feelings. Many coming to me for help in a state of desperation have said, "I know I am supposed to be saved, but I don't feel any different. I just don't feel saved." Wigglesworth knew that we are not to worry about feelings, that we are to feed on the Word of God. Feelings change, and a Christian's feelings may continue to fluctuate for a time. But the Word of God never changes, and eventually the Word of God will govern the feelings. Someone has said, "Faith in the Word is the root. Feelings are the fruit." If you tend the root well, you need have no fear about the fruit.

Not long ago a meeting was being held in the town hall of a certain city in England. In the foyer of the hall was a large display of religious books for sale. A friend of mine, wanting a Bible, approached one of the attendants.

"I would like to purchase a Bible," he said, "but there are none on display."

The young man responded, "Oh, we don't sell Bibles. We don't need them now; we have the Spirit."

We must question any experience, no matter how plausible it may seem, that does not have the Word of God as its basis.

Wigglesworth openly condemned basing belief on any experience which excluded the Word of God. To him the Word of God was supreme. Because some people had the foresight to record the life and teachings of great men and women like Smith Wigglesworth, thousands of people have been blessed and inspired.

Wigglesworth used to say that nothing substituted for the Word of God. One reason why he was able to minister as he did was that he lived in the Word and the Word lived in him. Because it lived in him, he was able to minister life.

Wigglesworth spoke the Word of Life into sightless eyes, and they saw; into deaf ears, and they heard; into the mouths of the mute, and they spoke.

He spoke the Word of Life into withered limbs, and they throbbed with new life; into disease-ridden bodies, and they surged with health.

He spoke the Word of Life to the demon-possessed, and the ministers of death had to flee.

He spoke the Word of Life to dead bodies, and they felt the power of resurrection life.

Wigglesworth spared no effort in trying to understand the power of God's Word. As far as he was concerned, time spent reading other books was wasted because it would be better spent reading God's Word.

Wigglesworth truly was a man of the Word. He recognized that one of the ministries of the Holy Spirit was to teach. But as for the intellectual approach to teaching, he certainly had reservations. He said on numerous occasions, "Some people like to read the Bible in Hebrew. Some like to read it in Greek. But I like to read it in the Holy Ghost."

When Peter and John stood before the religious hierarchy to answer the charges arising out of the healing of the lame man, the Bible says that when the council *perceived that they were unlearned and ignorant men, they marvelled; and they took knowledge of them, that they had been with Jesus.* (Acts 4:13). Obviously the Savior had left His mark upon them.

In the same way. It was evident Who had been Wigglesworth's teacher. In his interpretation of Scripture, without knowing one word of Hebrew or Greek, he often brought out thoughts from the background of these languages that left the scholars astounded. More than one said, "What kind of man is this?"

Had he been without the anointing, Wigglesworth would have been unpleasant to hear; but of the many times I have listened to him, whether in large or small gatherings or in private conversation, I have never known him to speak without the anointing.

Since he had never read any theological theses, his mind was never cluttered with confusing theories. It was always open to the Holy Spirit, and the revelation he received was tremendous. Before he slept, the last thing he did was to fill his mind with the pure Word of God. During sleep his subconscious mind had the wholesome Word of God to work upon. Often he awoke with some precious gem of thought.

Upon awakening, he turned again to the Word of God. He said it was important to get God's Word into his mind before the world could invade it. There is a saying which sums up his attitude toward God's Word: "God said it. I believe it. That settles it."

This was the standard by which Smith Wigglesworth lived and ministered. He never wavered even to the end. He did not die as we understand it. Nothing about him savored of death. He just went to heaven.

A Man of Compassion and Conviction

Wigglesworth loved people and displayed great concern for those in need. James Salter tells of an occasion when he accompanied Wigglesworth who was traveling to London for a ministry engagement. At Kings Cross Station in London, they boarded a bus for their final destination. There were only two vacant seats, one at the rear and the other at the front. Wigglesworth said to Salter, "You sit there," indicating the nearby rear seat. (The entrance and exit of London buses are at the rear.)

Wigglesworth went to the front to sit. He took out his New Testament and stood up among the passengers. In a clear voice he said, "Listen to this." Then he read a portion of Scripture. He explained very simply the Word of Life. James Salter later told me, "It made a tremendous impression on those people. Many were weeping. Wigglesworth walked down the aisle laying hands on people and praying for them. Who apart from him would dare to do such a thing on a public transport vehicle!"

With his God, Smith Wigglesworth was as bold as a lion.

On another occasion Wigglesworth boarded a train at Bradford to travel to London. He selected a corner seat. Eventually, five more people joined him in the compartment. As was his custom, he took out his Testament and began to read and pray silently. He never spoke a word to his fellow travelers. About thirty miles away from London he went to the rest room.

As he was making his way back to the compartment, the man who had been sitting next to him said, "I don't know what it was, but when I sat next to you, a terrible fear gripped me. I was afraid I was going to die. What was it?"

Wigglesworth said, "Come back into the compartment."

All the others there said they had experienced the same feeling. Wigglesworth explained to them about conviction and the way of salvation. They all knelt on the floor of the compartment and accepted the Lord.

Wigglesworth ministered this way on several occasions. He lived for opportunities such as these, seeing a potential in every person he met. He knew when to speak to people, or when to keep silent and wait for the Holy Spirit to first do His work. **He carried conviction with him, but with that he also carried a compassion which one could literally feel.** To be a successful soulwinner—which Wigglesworth certainly was—possessing both qualities is essential.

Once while I was visiting in his home, his daughter Alice told me about one of Wigglesworth's remarkable experiences. As he was opening his mail, he read a brief letter which seemed to stir him to the depth of his soul. All it said was, "Please come. We are in sore trouble." With tears running down his face, Wigglesworth handed the letter to Alice. It didn't convey anything to her.

"Why, Dad," she remarked, "you receive hundreds of letters asking for help. What is so different about this one?"

Without explaining, he said abruptly, "I will have to go," and, putting on his coat and hat, he set off for the address indicated on the letter.

He reached the address, that of a large house—a palatial dwelling by British standards—and rang the doorbell. The distinguished looking man who opened the door had a look of sadness on his countenance. Wigglesworth introduced himself in his customary manner: "I am Wigglesworth. I got your letter." The man held out his hand and invited him in.

Later, Wigglesworth said, "He took me by the arm, led me across a beautifully carpeted hall and up a flight of steps, never speaking a word. At the top of the stairs he opened a door, indicated to me to go into the room, then closed the door behind me." The man did not go in.

Wigglesworth saw something he would never forget: three strong men trying to hold down a lovely girl about seventeen years of age who was totally naked. The men could not hold her; she was a raging demoniac.

The girl's father, being a wealthy man, did not want his daughter locked away in a padded cell. Rather than institutionalize her, he kept her at home and employed these men to see that she did not destroy herself.

Suddenly the girl became aware of Wigglesworth's presence and ceased her raging. Glaring at him, she said, "I know who you are. You are Wigglesworth, the servant of the Most High God." What a commendation for devils to acknowledge the man of God!

Wigglesworth said, "Shut up, in the name of the Lord Jesus Christ." The girl backed away into the far corner of the room, and Wigglesworth followed her.

The girl, looking at Wigglesworth with an awful stare, snarled, "She is ours!"

Wigglesworth said, "I'm not here to argue with you, you foul spirits. Come out of her and trouble her no more." With a hideous scream, twelve devils came out of the girl.

Immediately the girl became aware that she was unclothed and, crying out, fled from the room. The men started to follow her, but Wigglesworth called them back and explained what had happened. Ten minutes later he heard a bedroom door open and close, and the sound of light footsteps tripping down the stairs. Wigglesworth then went downstairs and joined for tea a father, a mother, and one of the sweetest girls one could ever imagine—a girl who fifteen minutes before had been a raving maniac.

After returning home, he told his daughter, "Alice, what a lovely sight it was. How wonderful Jesus is!"

Often people have asked me what I consider to be the secret of Wigglesworth's power. There were several aspects. **One secret was his love and compassion for those in need.** What does the Bible say about Jesus?

> *But when he saw the multitudes, he was moved with compassion on them, because they fainted, and were scattered abroad, as sheep having no shepherd.*
>
> *Matthew 9:36*

> *And there came a leper to him, beseeching him, and kneeling down to him, and saying unto him, If thou wilt, thou canst make me clean.*
>
> *And Jesus, moved with compassion, put forth his hand, and touched him, and saith unto him, I will; be thou clean.*
>
> *Mark 1:40,41*

The hymn writer put it well when he penned these words: "Jesus, Thou art all compassion; pure unbounded love Thou art."

Wigglesworth was a man of compassion.

A Man of Prayer

Wigglesworth was moved with compassion toward the sinner, the sick, the oppressed, the demon-possessed, because he spent so much time in the presence of his Lord that he was like Him.

Someone once asked Wigglesworth if he regularly spent long seasons in prayer. He answered, "I don't very often spend more than a half hour in prayer at one time, but I never go more than a half hour without praying." **Prayer was his life. It was what he liked best of all. It was one of the secrets of his power.**

When people received healing under Wigglesworth's ministry, it was not merely a result of God's answering prayer because often, instead of saying a

41

prayer for the needy, Wigglesworth spoke the Word to them.

When Peter and John went to pray at the temple, they were confronted with the desperate need of the man who was lame from birth, laid at the gate of the temple to beg for alms. This man was expecting to receive some monetary contribution from Peter and John. Instead, they said, *Look on us* (Acts 3:4).

We perhaps would have said, "What kind of presumption is this? Who are these guys anyway? They surely have some nerve." But then Peter spoke these remarkable words:

> *Silver and gold have I none; but such as I have give I thee: in the name of Jesus Christ of Nazareth rise up and walk.*
>
> *And he took him by the right hand, and lifted him up: and immediately his feet and ankle bones received strength.*
>
> *And he leaping up stood, and walked.*
>
> Acts 3:6-8

Note the words *such as I have give I thee* (v. 6). This is the ministry of impartation. Wigglesworth ministered on this level.

He once told me a wonderful experience he had while staying in the home of a curate of the Church of England. He and the curate were sitting together talking after supper. No doubt the subject of their conversation was that the poor fellow had no legs. Artificial limbs in those days were unlike the sophisticated limbs of today.

Wigglesworth said to the man quite suddenly (which he often did when ministering in cases like this), "Go and get a pair of new shoes in the morning."

The poor fellow thought it was some kind of joke. However, after Wigglesworth and the curate had retired to their respective rooms for the night, God said to the curate, "Do as My servant hath said." What a designation for any person—*My servant!* God was identifying Himself with Wigglesworth.

There was no more sleep for the man that night. He rose up early, went downtown, and stood waiting for the shoe shop to open. The manager eventually arrived and opened the shop for business. The curate went in and sat down.

Presently an assistant came and said, "Good morning, sir. Can I help you?"

The man said, "Yes, would you get me a pair of shoes, please?"

"Yes, sir. Size and color?"

The man hesitated. The assistant then saw his condition and said, "Sorry, sir. We can't help you."

"It is all right, young man. But I do want a pair of shoes. Size 8, color black."

The assistant went to get the requested shoes. A few minutes later he returned and handed them to the man. The man put one stump into a shoe, and instantly a foot and leg formed! Then the same thing happened with the other leg!

He walked out of that shop, not only with a new pair of shoes, but also with a new pair of legs!

Wigglesworth was not surprised. He had expected this result. He often made remarks like this: "As far as God is concerned, there is no difference between forming a limb and healing a broken bone."

The point is this: Wigglesworth did not pray for the man; he told him what to do and the man did it.

One might think that the raising of the dead would be the greatest of all miracles. However, the Apostle Paul addressing King Agrippa said, *Why should it be thought a thing incredible with you, that God should raise the dead?* (Acts 26:8). I know of fourteen occasions when the dead were raised during Wigglesworth's ministry. Sometimes he would pray; but other times he would just speak the Word. The following are descriptions of two cases in which the dead were raised.

Wigglesworth went to a home in which the family was mourning the loss of a little boy, five years of age. In those days at a person's death, the body was not taken to a funeral home as is done today. The custom was to keep the body in the family home where friends could go pay their last respects.

Wigglesworth stood looking at the boy lying in his coffin as the father removed the cloth from the boy's face. Tears ran down Wigglesworth's cheeks as he saw the ravages of sin wreaked upon this innocent young victim lying cold in death. He requested that the father leave him alone in the room. He locked the door behind the father; then he lifted the still form of the lad from the coffin and stood it up in the corner of the room. Wigglesworth rebuked death in the name of the Lord Jesus, and commanded it to surrender its victim. The amazing miracle occurred: The child returned to life. When Wigglesworth lifted the body of the child out of the casket, he had no doubts as to the outcome.

On another occasion a dear friend of mine and a close friend of Wigglesworth's, who was the pastor of a church in England, told me of a man in his area who had died. Wigglesworth was called in. When he prayed, the man was raised from the dead. When he returned to life, however, he was still suffering from the disease which had killed him. Wigglesworth told the family that unless they repented and put matters right within their home, the man would die again. As a result, the family repented. Wigglesworth prayed for them, and the Lord healed the man, who lived for thirty more years.

Wigglesworth entered into a person's suffering. Often a physically strong person finds it difficult to relate to weakness and suffering, but this was not the case with Wigglesworth. Though he was a strong man physically, he was able to do so because he was strong in God. **Wigglesworth reveals the secret of his strength in God in the following statement: "I could not recollect a time when I did not long for God. I was always seeking Him. As a young lad, I would kneel down and ask Him to help me."**

What Wigglesworth was in God did not happen suddenly. He developed into it over a period of years. In his process of development he did not have it easy. He faced not only physical trials, but also persecution from other so-called Christians.

But despite the difficulties Wigglesworth had to face, particularly the persecution he faced on the European continent, he always remained motivated by his love for people, his abhorrence of the ravages of sin, and his overwhelming passion to know the Lord.

A Man of Faith

The following incidents, which Wigglesworth faced in the early part of his ministry, illustrate his great faith.

He was asked to pray for a young woman who was oppressed with an evil power. At the house, he was taken to the room where she was. When he saw her, Wigglesworth was moved with compassion. Some of the people present were holding her down on the bed. Her husband was also there, holding a little baby.

The whole atmosphere was charged with satanic power. Out of the corner of his eye, Wigglesworth noticed another young woman creeping out of the room. The look in her eyes was dreadful. "I knew I was facing demonic activity," he later related. "Something had to be done."

He said, "My faith began to penetrate the heavens. If you want anything from God, you will have to pray into heaven. That is where it all is. If you live in the earth realm and expect to receive from God, you will never get anything.

"I saw in the presence of God the limitations of my faith. Then there came another faith—a faith that takes the promise, a faith that believes God's Word. And from that presence, I came back to earth a different man. God gave me a faith that could shake heaven."

In that faith he wrought total deliverance for that young wife. After sleeping for fourteen hours, she awoke perfectly healed because Wigglesworth had been moved from the natural to the supernatural. He did not have to wait for God when faced with an emergency. He already knew God.

What a power this man had with God. Many times he battled with unbelief and emerged victorious. Once a group of young men were questioning him. One of them asked, "How can one possess a great faith?" Wigglesworth answered very simply, "First the blade, then the ear, then the corn in the ear." (Mark 4:28.) That was all he said, but what an answer! It was packed with profound Holy Ghost theology. He simply meant that faith was a consistent progression, going on to perfection. Faith comes from knowing more of God every day.

Wigglesworth never became involved in theological debates or scriptural interpretations. He knew nothing of the theological jargon with which Bible students are so familiar. But he certainly knew his God, which is far more important!

A Man of Love

Wigglesworth's unaltering love of the Lord increased with every passing day. To him, the Lord was everything that made for real life. As a result he could love his fellow men with the same passion that he loved the Lord.

The way he portrayed this love, however, was misunderstood at times by observers. During certain times of ministry, Wigglesworth faced opposition from these observers. Wigglesworth viewed this not as a personal criticism but rather a criticism of the work of God. He maintained that any attack upon the work of God originated with the Devil. James Salter told me of one such incident that occurred as he was accompanying Wigglesworth in his ministry.

Often in his meetings Wigglesworth would say, "I want the person with the worst case of sickness in this place to stand up."

"Not having the faith of my father-in-law," Salter related, "I was often fearful."

At one particular meeting that Salter described, Wigglesworth gave the usual invitation as soon as he came to the platform. Sitting between two other ladies on the front row was a woman who was desperately ill. The two ladies had almost carried her into the place and were supporting her as they sat there. At the invitation, these two friends struggled to get the woman on her feet.

Wigglesworth said, "Bring her here."

With difficulty they managed to get her to the platform.

Instead of praying for her as everyone expected him to do, Wigglesworth, in his broad Yorkshire dialect, told them, "Let go of her. Let her stand by herself." When the ladies did as he said, the woman crashed to the floor.

Wigglesworth was unmoved. "Pick her up," he told them.

They did as he said, and again he ordered them to let her stand alone. Reluctantly they complied and once more the poor woman fell down with a thud.

"Pick her up," Wigglesworth said. Again, they did as he told them.

By this time some people in the congregation were becoming hostile, but Wigglesworth paid no attention.

"Let go of her," he said to the two ladies, but this time they would not.

"You callous brute!" a man in the congregation cried out. Wigglesworth looked right at the man and said, "You mind your own business. I know my business!"

Turning to the two women, he repeated his command: "Let go of her and let her stand by herself. Do as I say!"

With trepidation they did so, but this time the woman did not fall. There on the platform beside her lay a big cancer which had come away from her.

"I think Wigglesworth adequately proved his point," Salter told me.

In such cases, Wigglesworth was invariably right. He knew his God well enough to know that beyond all doubt, God would not fail him in a situation like that. When he told that congregation, "I know my business," he was on the hot line—in touch with the throne room. I knew Wigglesworth well enough to know that he was not angry with the man who hurled abuse at him. He was angry at the Devil! Wigglesworth was sorry for the man. I also know that he would not have shown the slightest sign of elation when God vindicated him to the embarrassment of the man.

Wigglesworth loved people; but when the work of God was being attacked, he would vehemently defend it, no matter where the attack came from.

A Man of Courage and Peace

The only anger Smith Wigglesworth ever exhibited was against the Devil. He experienced divine visitation more than once. He testified to not only feeling God's presence, but also seeing Him as a living person. He also experienced satanic visitation, but he was never afraid of the Devil.

On one occasion Wigglesworth awoke during the night aware of a satanic presence. Looking across the room, he saw the Devil himself standing there. Wigglesworth said to Satan, "Oh, it's only you." Then he turned over and went back to sleep.

This was not an imaginary experience as some might think. Wigglesworth never tried to be dramatic; he was too much of a realist. He never exaggerated or altered a word in his testimony. He always reported the absolute truth because he loved Him Who is the truth. He never did or said anything which would grieve his Lord.

Some might think that Wigglesworth's life must have been one continual strain, but this is not so. Few people relaxed more than he did; relaxation to him was being in the presence of his Lord. He was so relaxed that he was alive to every opportunity that presented itself. He had learned the secret of Isaiah 26:3: *Thou wilt keep him in perfect peace, whose mind is stayed on thee: because he trusteth in thee.*

The words *perfect peace* in the Hebrew literally mean "peace peace." In other words, *perfect peace* is "double peace," or "a double portion of peace."

Wigglesworth faced every circumstance with absolute calm.

2

Smith Wigglesworth
The Spirit

The frustration from making an assessment of what we are in God, and comparing it with what we could be, often breeds within us an inferiority complex. The devastating effect this can have upon our lives is not helpful to us or to our fellow man, nor is it glorifying to God. **We may be nothing, but in God we can be mighty. Wigglesworth's knowledge of this spiritual secret is what set him apart from many others who might have possessed greater natural ability or capacity.**

It would be interesting to know how many ministers of the Gospel have been inspired by Smith Wigglesworth. A great number in the United States, especially, seem to have been blessed and inspired by his ministry. And through the years, I have known or met countless Britons who have testified to the inspiration they have received through the ministry of this remarkable man of God.

At this hour a great need exists for men and women to arise—men and women who have learned the secret of real faith, who know the Lord as Wigglesworth knew Him, and who are willing to commit themselves to the ministry without reservation as Wigglesworth did.

Wigglesworth's dedication was tested, as we have seen. He was tested physically and spiritually throughout his long and fruitful career. However, all that he went through only instilled in him a determination to be more like Jesus.

If groups which preach lifeless, erroneous doctrines can make inroads into human society through sheer dedication, how much more should the true child of God moving in the power of the Holy Ghost be able to accomplish? This calls for serious heart searching on the part of Christians.

In Romans 12:1,2 we see the principle by which Smith Wigglesworth lived:

> *I beseech you therefore, brethren, by the mercies of God, that ye present your bodies a living sacrifice, holy, acceptable unto God, which is your reasonable service.*
>
> *And be not conformed to this world: but be ye transformed by the renewing of your mind, that ye may prove what is that good, and acceptable, and perfect, will of God.*

A Spirit of Calm

In all the years I knew Smith Wigglesworth, he was always the same. To him moods were a thing of the past, belonging to the "old Wigglesworth."

Wigglesworth had learned the secret which the Apostle John had learned while on the isle of Patmos, cut off from the fellowship he so greatly treasured. This secret is found in Revelation 1:10. John writes: *I was in the Spirit on the Lord's day.* It was while in this attitude that John caught a vision of the risen, glorified Christ.

The result was simply this: John learned how insignificant earth's circumstances are when compared with heaven's provision. Once a person has learned this truth, no circumstance can ever again alarm him or her.

Wigglesworth, I believe, had learned the secret of seeing earth's circumstances from heaven's standpoint. Whether the circumstance was death, demon possession, or anything else, Wigglesworth met each occasion with a calmness known only to those who know God well and who are living in the realm of the Holy Ghost. Wigglesworth lived in victory because he lived in the Spirit.

Someone ably said of Wigglesworth that he learned the secret of giving to God in worship what was His due and of giving to man in ministry what was his need. This statement sums up the spirit of the man, Wigglesworth.

A Spirit of Discernment

It was evident throughout Wigglesworth's ministry that he knew the mind of the Spirit.

As a young man I felt it was the call of God for me to go to Africa as a missionary. This conclusion was confirmed by every event. One day sitting opposite to me in his home, Wigglesworth said, "You will not go to Africa as a missionary; it is not God's will for you."

"But every circumstance points to it. The door is open."

"That may be," he responded. "But the door will close. You mark my words."

I waited. Before many weeks had passed, the door closed and closed so tightly that any possibility of its reopening did not exist. Wigglesworth's words came to pass because he knew the mind of God.

Often people have said that one person does not know God's will for another. There are exceptions to this rule, however, and this case was one. Even though the evidence seemed conclusive that God's will was for me to go to Africa, Wigglesworth knew I was not to go; and God's will did prove to be otherwise.

One could also see that Wigglesworth knew the mind of the Spirit from the way he discerned with unerring accuracy the source of a person's affliction. In one meeting, Wigglesworth ministered to two people who seemed to everyone but Wigglesworth to have identical problems: Both were deaf and dumb.

Wigglesworth put is fingers into the first person's deaf ears and said, "Be opened in Jesus' name." He then placed his hand on the person's lips and said, "Tongue, be loosed." The man was healed.

But he dealt with the second person in a different manner. He looked the man straight in the eye and said, "Thou deaf and dumb spirit, come out, in the name of the Lord Jesus!" The person was wonderfully delivered.

Later Wigglesworth explained, "You don't lay hands on the Devil. You have nothing to impart to him. You rebuke him and tell him to go. But you have to be in the right place with God to do that."

A Spiritual Hunger and Thirst for God

One might wonder how Wigglesworth attained that standard, that "right place with God" to which he referred. In response, let me begin by relating Wigglesworth's account of how he received salvation.

At the age of eight, Wigglesworth attended a little Methodist church with his grandmother. He remembered them gathering around the small, old-fashioned combustion stove in the middle of the church and singing the old hymns, as only the old Methodists could sing:

Oh, the Lamb, the Bleeding Lamb,
  the Lamb of Calvary;
The Lamb that was slain, that liveth again,
  to intercede for me.

They were dancing around the old stove, faces alight with the Glory of God, when Wigglesworth became conscious of the Spirit of God drawing nigh. At that time he realized that Jesus was his Savior and was born again.

From then on, Wigglesworth never had any doubts as to whether he was saved. To him the experience was so positive because he had begun at an early age to not countenance half measures. Anything he could not entirely devote himself to, he would prefer not to do at all. This trait was characteristic of him to the very last. He could never imagine salvation as an alloy. To him it was pure—unadulterated by any worldly additions. Also because of that trait, he refused to be content with anything less than all of the blessings of salvation to which man was entitled.

As a result, he had an insatiable hunger for God. He was far from being discontented. The more he had of God, the more he wanted. The words on a card someone once sent me well sum up Wigglesworth's thoughts on the matter:

All of self, none of God.
Less of self, more of God.
None of self, all of God.

Hungry for all that God had, Wigglesworth waited upon God until he was transformed and cleansed of self. He was conscious that God's plan for His people involved power. The idea of a weak, insipid Christian did not seem right to him; he could not visualize it. He was aware of spiritual growth. He did not question stages of development; but set as his standard to attain, regardless of the cost, the ultimate goal of being like Christ.

Wigglesworth could not accept the idea of engaging in God's work without adequate power to do God's will. In his search for God he heard of the outpouring of the Spirit of God in the All Saints Anglican Church in Sunderland.

He decided to go there, especially when he heard that people were being baptized with the Holy Ghost, as on the day of Pentecost. He thought he had already been baptized with the Holy Ghost because of his previous teaching, but could not understand where tongues fit. When he reached the church at Sunderland, he told them he wanted to hear the tongues.

The people there said to him, "What you need is the baptism with the Holy Spirit," but he replied, "I have already had the baptism of the Holy Ghost."

Later, he told me, "I saw that these people were earnest, godly people, but I argued with them on this matter of tongues."

Wigglesworth disputed sharply with one missionary. But afterwards he prayed a whole night with the man. He then spent the following four days with him. "After that four days," Wigglesworth told me, "I wanted nothing but God."

His mind, however, turned to practical matters. He told his host that he needed to return home to attend to his business and family. Before leaving, he went to the minister's wife and said, "I'm going home now, but I have not yet received the tongues."

"It's not the tongues you need," she replied. "It's the baptism with the Holy Ghost."

"I have had the baptism." He still looked upon the baptism with the Holy Ghost and speaking with tongues as two separate experiences. But in his hunger for the things of God, Wigglesworth said, "I would like for you to lay hands on me."

God saw the longing of Smith's soul, and as His Word says, *He satisfieth the longing soul* (Ps. 107:9). Wigglesworth said later, "The fire fell. I was clean. I saw a vision of Jesus. I saw the dross.* I saw the empty

---

*"worthless matter separated from the better part"

tomb. I spoke with other tongues. I knew then that at that time I had been baptized with the Holy Ghost.''

When relating this testimony, he added, ''If we knew the blessing of being filled with the Third Person of the Trinity, we would set aside everything else, to tarry for His fullness.''

A Spirit of Holiness

Wigglesworth believed that as the temples of the Holy Ghost we should be clean, and that we should never allow anything to defile that temple of our bodies. Paul said to the Corinthians concerning this matter:

> *What? know ye not that your body is the temple of the Holy Ghost which is in you, which ye have of God, and ye are not your own?*
>
> *For ye are bought with a price: therefore glorify God in your body, and in your spirit, which are God's.*
>
> *1 Corinthians 6:19,20*

To Wigglesworth, it was an awesome privilege for his body to be the temple of the Holy Ghost. He nourished his spiritual life through his communion with God, by living in touch with God. When a child of God ceases to hunger after righteousness and purity, Wigglesworth maintained, Satan gets in. He once remarked, ''When I catch the first breath of the

Spirit, I leave everything and everybody to be in His presence, to hear what He has to say to me." He was very sensitive to the movings of God's Spirit.

Quite often I hear people say, "God has told me . . . " Knowing how some people live, I am fearful when I hear that comment. I was never fearful when I heard Wigglesworth say that because he rarely said it. He had no need to. Whatever he said had come to him from God. Everything he was and did resulted from the moving of God's Spirit.

In his prayer life he often prayed in the Spirit. He did this because he said things which are too deep for our minds to grasp and too profound for our language to utter. These can only be appropriated by our spirits. When Wigglesworth gave an utterance in the Spirit, he interpreted it very often. On many occasions I heard him do this. Each instance was an unforgettable experience. The interpretations were absolutely profound.

Through the years the validity of this practice has been questioned, but it is quite scriptural: *Wherefore let him that speaketh in an unknown tongue pray that he may interpret* (1 Cor. 14:13). I see no grounds for dissension.

When I heard Smith Wigglesworth interpreting his own utterance, I was aware that it was coming directly from the heart of God. One proof of this was a change in his language.

Since Wigglesworth was a man with no education, his grammar was very poor. However, when he interpreted his own utterance, he spoke English grammar of the highest standard. Without doubt, this occurrence was miraculous. **Through learning the secret of praying in the Spirit, Wigglesworth touched realms far beyond himself.**

What Paul wrote about in 1 Corinthians 14:14,15 Smith Wigglesworth learned by experience:

For if I pray in an unknown tongue, my spirit prayeth, but my understanding is unfruitful.

What is it then? I will pray with the spirit, and I will pray with the understanding also: I will sing with the spirit, and I will sing with the understanding also.

One could often see a change in Wigglesworth as he prayed. He would continue speaking in an unknown tongue as he moved into another realm. He often prayed this way when faced with a desperate need. It was an application of Romans 8:26,27 which says:

Likewise the Spirit also helpeth our infirmities: for we know not what we should pray for as we ought: but the Spirit itself maketh intercession for us with groanings which cannot be uttered.

And he that searcheth the hearts knoweth what is the mind of the Spirit, because he maketh intercession for the saints according to the will of God.

The Christian Church needs to learn the secret that Smith Wigglesworth learned and walked in: this secret of praying in the Spirit.

A Spirit of Humility

Wigglesworth knew the danger of pride. He never let it invade the sanctity of his communion with God. To do this, he took Communion every day, keeping Calvary ever in sight as an antidote against pride. *For as often as ye eat this bread, and drink this cup, ye do shew the Lord's death till he come* (1 Cor. 11:26). Often he would be alone with his Lord as he took the bread and the wine, emblems of the broken body and the shed blood of Jesus.

One wonders what percentage of Christians takes of the bread and wine without a thought as to the tremendous importance and implications of their act. Many take it merely out of habit or because of tradition. The partaking of Communion is so serious an issue that it can mean either judgment or blessing, depending upon the attitude with which it is taken.

Wigglesworth partook of the emblems with the utmost sincerity, fully alive to his responsibility. As a result, he lived in unbroken communion with his Lord. Because of this, he was always ready for service, never taken by surprise. He often said, ''If you have to stop to get ready when an opportunity arises, you are too late. The opportunity is gone and the chances are that it will not be presented again.''

With this attitude, Wigglesworth was never at a loss for what to do in any situation. An illustration follows.

The pastor of a particular church where Wigglesworth was ministering asked Wigglesworth to go with him to visit a member of his church, a lady who was sick. Wigglesworth agreed. When they reached the house, it was evident to Wigglesworth that the woman was a person of considerable means.

The two ministers were taken to a room where the woman was lying in bed. Several bottles containing various kinds of pills were on the nightstand near her.

The pastor said, ''We have come to pray for you.'' But Wigglesworth, looking at the woman, said, ''I haven't. You are enjoying that sickness. You don't want prayer.'' With those words, he walked from the room and back to the car to wait for the pastor.

After consoling the woman, the pastor, with a very distressed look on his face, joined Wigglesworth in the car. He said, ''You have done the church a great disservice. That dear sister contributes a lot of money to us.''

Wigglesworth retorted, "Aye, that's the trouble."

"Well," said the pastor, "I don't suppose we shall see her again."

"Oh, she'll be back, and very soon." Wigglesworth's reply was very calm.

They went to the pastor's home for tea, then to church for the evening service.

The lady who had been sick in bed that afternoon walked into the service. She came forward for prayer. Wigglesworth asked, "Are you ready now?"

"Yes, I am."

Then she added, "After you left this afternoon, I was convicted that what you said was true."

That evening, she was healed.

A Spirit of Worship and Ministry

In his communion with God, Wigglesworth learned the secret of worship. Very often, we try to work up worship, causing it to be very mechanical. True worship comes down into the spirit. From that fountain within, the volume of worship which comes from the very depths of our being springs forth.

Wigglesworth learned from experience what Jesus meant when He said: *But the hour cometh, and now is, when the true worshippers shall worship the Father in spirit and in truth: for the father seeketh such to worship him. God is a Spirit: and they that worship him must worship him in spirit and in truth* (John 4:23,24).

The worship that Wigglesworth offered was truly in spirit and in truth . It was born out of the depths of his experiences (and he certainly went through his times of testing).

In his communion with God, Wigglesworth learned the secret and the importance of the ministry of impartation which includes the laying on of hands. Wigglesworth, however, carried the ministry of impartation a step further. He could impart without the laying on of hands.

Down the hill from Wigglesworths home was the beautiful Manningham Park, a public park with lovely flower gardens. I cannot pass b that place today without remembering Wigglesworth and the people he blessed there.

When he was home, it was usual for him to go to the park and sit for a while. Often someone else would sit down on the same bench. Without speaking, Wigglesworth imparted something to whoever was sitting there. If the person was unsaved, as was often the case, Wigglesworth would pray silently for him to come under conviction and get saved.

Whatever the need might be, Wigglesworth could perceive it. He had no need to question anyone; people were drawn to him by the Spirit. Before long, almost without realizing it, a person would be pouring out his heart to Smith. Everyone went away blessed. Wigglesworth always said, "If you don't minister life, you will minister death and leave folks worse off than when you found them."

Being in a "receiving meeting" with Wigglesworth was quite an experience. He did not call them "tarrying meetings" as some did. He would tell the people, "You don't tarry for the Holy Ghost. He has already been given; He is here. You don't tarry; you receive."

After he had the people sit down, he would tell them to receive by faith, then to speak out. "I will count to five," he would say. "When I get to five, then do as I have told you to do." When he reached five, people would begin speaking in tongues. It was like waves rolling throughout the place.

Wigglesworth maintained that there was a difference between preaching and ministering. Paul, an apostle of Jesus Christ by the will of God, refers to himself as a minister. Writing to the Romans, he speaks with utmost clarity on this subject: *For I long to see you, that I may impart unto you some spiritual gift, to the end ye may be established* (Rom. 1:11). Again, in 1 Thessalonians 2:8 he writes: . . . *we were willing to have imparted unto you, not the gospel of God only, but also our own souls, because ye were dear unto us.*

This impartation of which Paul speaks is a giving out of the Spirit. One cannot give out if there is nothing to give out. From this you can see Wigglesworth's point: If you don't minister or impart life, you will minister death.

The calling to be a Christian carries with it an awful responsibility. We cannot live unto ourselves. Wigglesworth made it clear that whether it is to adults or to children, whatever the circumstance, if we are living right, we can minister the Spirit by faith. If we are not getting the results we ought to, we should examine our hearts to find out why. John wrote to the early believers: *Beloved, if our heart condemn us not, then have we confidence toward God. And whatsoever we ask, we receive of him, because we keep his commandments, and do those things that are pleasing in his sight* (1 John 3:21,22).

The standard is high, but we must remember that the believer's ministry is potentially far-reaching. And Smith Wigglesworth's ministry was certainly far-reaching.

It is said that when he visited San Francisco, so many people wanted to hear him that he preached and ministered by walking the streets. The people brought out their sick and laid them on mattresses so that the shadow of Wigglesworth could pass over them. As it did, the sick were healed. This is New Testament ministry, for we read in Acts 5:15, *They brought forth the sick into the streets, and laid them on beds and couches, that at the least the shadow of Peter passing by might overshadow some of them.* Wigglesworth proved that the apostles' ministry, as commissioned by Jesus did not cease with their deaths, but is operative until it has fulfilled its given purpose.

Because of what has happened in the Church through the centuries, some people have concluded that this type of New Testament ministry has ceased. Examine the mandate Jesus gives in Mark 16:15-18:

> *And he said unto them* (the disciples), *Go ye into all the world, and preach the gospel to every creature. He that believeth and is baptized shall be saved; but he that believeth not shalt be damned.*
>
> *And these signs shall follow them that believe; In my name shall they cast out devils; they shall speak with new tongues; they shall take up serpents; and if they drink any deadly thing, it shall not hurt them; they shall lay hands on the sick, and they shall recover.*

If, as some people suggest, the ministry of the supernatural ceased with the apostles, how do they explain that the twentieth-century man, Wigglesworth, ministered with the same power as did the apostles—even to the raising of the dead, the casting out of devils, the healing of the sick, and other creative miracles? Wigglesworth maintained steadfastly that every child of God holds the potential for the miraculous. The great question that filled his mind was this: Why did they not realize that potential?

There is evidence that at various times in history, some members of the Church have realized this potential. How do we rise to meet the challenge of the men and women of God who have left their mark for good upon the world? Developing characteristics and ministry similar to that of Smith Wigglesworth will aid in reaching this end. If just one person does so on the basis of reading these lines, it will have been worth my effort in writing them.

Wigglesworth's ears were always open to the Spirit and closed to the flesh. He used to say, "If the Holy Ghost doesn't move me, I move the Holy Ghost." This statement evoked a great deal of criticism by many people who considered it irreverent. But this was not so. Wigglesworth's fervent love for God was unmatched by those who criticized him.

Being in a meeting which Wigglesworth directed was an unforgettable experience. Whenever he came to my home church, my pastor left the meeting entirely to him.

The moment he entered the pulpit, Wigglesworth would say, "All those who want something from God, put up your hand." Hands would go up all over.

Then he would say, ''All those who are going to be blessed, put the other hand up.'' Nearly everybody would put up their other hand and have both hands in the air.

Next he would say, ''Keep those hands raised; and if you are going to take the blessing with you when you go home, stand up.'' Obeying, almost everyone would stand with both hands still raised.

Waves of glory would then sweep the congregation. The atmosphere was always electric. A multitude of needs were met during those times.

This is what Wigglesworth meant by moving in the Holy Ghost. None of his critics could question the moving of God's Spirit at such a gathering. Wigglesworth explained these occurrences this way: ''Faith moves first; then God moves in answer to faith.''

One of the special areas with which Smith Wigglesworth dealt was problem marriages. Wigglesworth always used God's methods, so the solutions were true and long lasting.

Once a lady came to Wigglesworth for help concerning her son's marriage. The young man had once loved the Lord and married a fine young woman, but after a time the young man backslid. His marriage deteriorated to the extent that he left his wife and moved back with his mother. The situation was difficult for the mother and greatly distressed her.

Wigglesworth said to the lady, "Give me your handkerchief." When she did, he put it between his hands and said, "Lord, smite this young man with conviction." Handing the kerchief back to the woman, he told her to put it under the young man's pillow and not tell him about it.

When the lady got home, her son was gone, so she did as Wigglesworth had told her. When her son returned, the hour was late and the lady was already in bed. After being home a while, the son went to his room, undressed, and got into bed. As soon as his head touched the pillow, he came under terrible conviction. Hastily, he got out of bed, fell on his knees, and got right with God. Then he dressed and called to his mother even though it was midnight.

"Don't worry, Mum. I'm going back home. I'll see you tomorrow." And away he went.

When he got home, he and his wife had a glorious reconciliation.

Numerous marriages were saved through Wigglesworth's ministry, but always through miraculous means because his approach was not tactful. Often it was the opposite, like that of a bull in a china shop. However, Wigglesworth was always earnest, and his infectious earnestness shone through like the sun shining through the clouds. Also, he had a love and a compassion which his rough exterior could not hide for very long. Soon after a couple had recovered from the initial shock of his approach, they would pour out their hearts to him. As he listened, tears would stream down his face. Every couple he counseled left with their problem solved.

In handling such cases, Christians often unwittingly tend toward the psychological approach. Human nature usually works that way. But Wigglesworth kept a ready ear for the voice of God. He wanted to hear what advice the Father had to give.

Wigglesworth had no special techniques. He was motivated only by the love of God in his soul. He knew that without it, techniques counted for nothing. He lived by the principles of 1 Corinthians 13:1,2:

> *Though I speak with the tongues of men and of angels, and have not love, I am become as sounding brass, or a tinkling cymbal.*

> *And though I have the gift of prophecy, and understand all mysteries, and all knowledge; and though I have all faith, so that I could remove mountains, and have not love, I am nothing.*

Smith Wigglesworth exhibited this principle in his life and ministry. The passage goes on to say, *Love suffereth long, and is kind* (v. 4). Love puts the best possible construction on any situation; it sees the potential for good in the very worst of characters. For this reason, love succeeds when everything else fails. This love was what brought much success in Wigglesworth's ministry.

A Soulwinning Spirit

If Wigglesworth ever attended an evangelistic college or enrolled in a correspondence course on how to win men for Christ, I knew nothing of it. In fact, it is doubtful that any existed then. In the primitive Methodist church of that day, a person's candidacy for the ministry was not dependent upon how many diplomas he held or how well he could preach, but upon how many souls he had won for Christ.

Wigglesworth had a passion for the souls of men! He and his wife spent every Saturday night in prayer, claiming at least fifty souls for Sunday. He knew they would get them, and they did.

Wigglesworth was not in the ministry then as we generally understand it. He and his wife were in the Salvation Army. But, truly, he was in the ministry from an early age.

As a boy, he won other boys to Christ. He could never understand how anybody who claimed to be a Christian could have a negative attitude toward the winning of souls. To Wigglesworth, seeking God's direction about where to go to win souls was the only valid soulwinning technique.

Divine direction is what soulwinning is all about and this is what Wigglesworth always sought. Rather than having his eyes on some manual of soulwinning techniques, he had his ears open to the voice of God. That paid dividends every time.

When Solomon was made king of Israel, the Lord appeared to him and said, *Ask what I shall give thee* (1 Kings 3:5). Solomon then magnified the Lord for allowing him to succeed his father David as king over Israel. But he said:

> *I am but a little child: I know not how to go out or come in.*
>
> *And thy servant is in the midst of thy people which thou hast chosen, a great people, that cannot be numbered nor counted for multitude.*
>
> *Give therefore thy servant an understanding heart to judge thy people.*
>
> 1 Kings 3:7-9

The word *understanding* in Hebrews means "hearing." Verse 9 then should read, *Give thy servant a hearing heart* or *a listening heart.* This is precisely what Wigglesworth had, which reveals why he had such confidence.

Personally, Wigglesworth did not understand what fear was. However, he was fearful about what he saw happening in the Church, particularly in regard to the souls of men. He would say, "Oh, what indifference there is concerning the souls of men. We are too much involved in trivialities, things that don't matter." He would say that the greatest need was for a burden for the lost. Lost souls were never far from his thoughts; he shed many tears on their behalf. These words of the Psalmist meant so much to him: *He that goeth forth and weepeth, bearing precious seed, shall doubtless come again with rejoicing, bringing his sheaves with him* (Ps. 126:6).

Whatever Wigglesworth did was out of love for his Lord. He never had as a motive the thought of reward. His great love for children was so evident that it did not take long for children to realize it. He used to go to Liverpool, then a great seaport, where he would gather the children and talk to them about Jesus. Because many of them were brought up in poverty, he would spend all his money to provide for them. Hundreds were brought to Christ.

He fasted every Sunday and could not remember seeing fewer than fifty souls saved. What a challenge to every Christian.

In all his personal contacts, he was always in the right place at the right time with the right word. His critics would say it was only coincidence, but it could hardly be coincidence so many times over. His personal contacts numbered in the thousands. **Wigglesworth's secret was that he was always in**

contact with the throne of God. He had no time for theological arguments because his one aim was to save the lost.

Wigglesworth once told me a story about an experience he had on a train, a good illustration of how God directed him in soulwinning. The train had stopped for a few minutes at a station. After taking a walk to stretch his legs, Wigglesworth returned to his compartment and found that he had company. A young woman and her mother had boarded while he had been out.

To the young woman, Wigglesworth said, "You look miserable."

"I have every reason to be," she replied. "I am going to the hospital to have my leg amputated."

"Do you know that Jesus can save you?" Wigglesworth said.

"What do you mean?"

Wigglesworth then talked to both women about the Savior. Before long, both of them had accepted the Lord Jesus Christ. He then said to the young woman, "The same Savior Who has saved your soul can heal your body. Can you believe that?"

"Yes," she replied.

"All right, then, I am going to pray for you."

He anointed her with oil, as he sometimes did, and prayed for her, in the name of Jesus. Then he said, ''Now go to the hospital. Let them examine the leg and show them that you don't need the operation.''

When she did as he said, she found that she had been miraculously healed. How remarkably Wigglesworth fit into God's plan! He had a marvelous set of ears which heard God's voice!

Wigglesworth gives another example of the way God directed him in soulwinning.

One time he felt that God wanted him to go out for some reason. Like Abraham, he went out not knowing whither he went. He wondered about every person he saw, as to whether that was the one to whom God wanted him to minister. This went on for some time without his getting any witness.

Suddenly when he saw a man driving a horse and cart, he felt God telling him to get on that cart. Like Philip of old who was sent to join the Ethiopian eunuch in his chariot, Wigglesworth obeyed.

Mounting beside the driver, he was met with a very hostile reception. Could he have made a mistake? No. Despite the man's initial threat to throw Wigglesworth off, by the time they had reached their destination, the man had wept his way to Calvary.

Only four days after this event occurred, Wigglesworth's mother asked her son, ''Did you speak to a man on a cart about his soul?''

"Yes, I did."

"His wife has been to see me. By the description her husband gave her, she thought it must have been you. She wanted you to know that he died yesterday."

It has been said that we cannot limit the Holy Ghost to a particular method. If we try to do so, we will find that we are then on our own, causing our accomplishment to be zero.

Because he was so sensitive to the voice of God's Spirit, Wigglesworth was unpredictable. He dealt differently with each one of the thousands of people to whom he witnessed. As each case was different from the others, so was his manner of approach. In his ministry to the sick, for instance, he anointed some with oil, others he laid hands on, and to others, he just spoke the Word. The results, however, were the same.

When he was asked about his methods of approaching people, Wigglesworth answered, "It all depends on what the Father has to say." His answer was the same when he was asked about the raising of the dead or the casting out of devils. He dealt with each case according to the directions he received from the Lord. When he directed a service, no one knew the direction it might take. Usually given a free hand, he always directed the services fearlessly.

As soon as he stood to start the meeting in one particular service, he said, "I want six people to pray. Just pray brief prayers. If you are in touch with heaven, it won't take twenty minutes to bring the blessing down."

A lady always the first in both prayer and testimony started to pray. It was evident that she was not going to deviate from her usual pattern of praying all around the world. Wigglesworth looked at her, then said suddenly, "Sit down, woman. Save the rest of that prayer until you get home. We don't want bedroom prayers here. Next please."

Normally, an action of that sort would bring a meeting into bondage—but not in a service Wigglesworth was convening. He knew the mind of the Spirit. When the next person stood to pray, the atmosphere was charged with the presence of God.

His critics would say, "He could have used a little diplomacy, at least." It is doubtful that Smith Wigglesworth knew what diplomacy meant. He simply addressed each situation as God told him to so that no one could misunderstand. Had he tried to be diplomatic, the atmosphere could well have been destroyed.

On another occasion, I was attending a meeting when a woman confined to a wheelchair, crippled with a severe arthritic condition, was brought in. Flannel material was fastened with safety pins all around her joints.

Looking at the flannel, Wigglesworth asked her, "What's this all about?"

"It's to keep my joints warm."

"Get it off. There's more pins in here than in an ironmonger's shop" (That's a hardware store.)

When the person who had brought her had taken all the material away from her joints, Wigglesworth said to the woman, "Get out of that chair."

"I can't."

"I didn't ask you if you could. I said, 'Get out of the chair.' "

She stood up.

"Now, walk."

She said again, "I can't."

"I didn't ask you if you could. I said, 'Walk.' "

"I can't."

Getting behind her, he gave her a push and shouted, "Walk, woman, walk!"

She walked for the first time in years!

Wigglesworth did not *explain* what he wanted her to do: He just *told* her by giving crisp, sharp commands. Despite what some may have thought, it worked and that was all that mattered.

Wigglesworth then said, "If there are any who want something from God, come up here and get it."

When a man walked to the front, Wigglesworth asked him, "What's up with you?"

"I have a very severe throat condition. I have had surgery for it, but have not been able to eat solid food for eleven years."

"How do you live, man?"

"Everything has to be made into a liquid form, then I can get it down."

Instead of praying for the man, Wigglesworth told him, "Go home. Tell your wife to cook you a good supper. Then eat it. I shall expect you to come tomorrow night and tell folks what God has done for you."

The man went home and did as Wigglesworth had said. The next night he came back and testified that he had eaten for the first time in eleven years!

Wigglesworth could take such bold and fearless actions for two reasons: He received his direction from the Spirit of God, and he directed all his actions toward the ultimate goad of soulwinning.

Once when he was taking an ocean voyage, Wigglesworth was approached by the person in charge of entertainment. After explaining to Wigglesworth that one of his projects was to explore the talents of the passengers, he asked, "Mr. Wigglesworth, would you be so kind as to take part in our program?"

"What would you like me to do?"

"Can you sing?"

"Well, it's not one of my specialties, but I would do that."

"Good, I will put you down to sing."

Then Wigglesworth added, "Only on the condition that I am first on the program."

"That will suit me fine."

When the time of the program arrived, Wigglesworth went to the ship's theater. After the opening welcome to all the passengers, the organizer said, "The first act is a song by Mr. Smith Wigglesworth from Bradford."

Smith stood and took a bow, then started to sing a Gospel song. As he sang, all the longings, compassion, and love of his heart shone through to that audience. Soon tears were not only in his eyes, but also in the eyes of all the people who heard him. His was the only item on that afternoon's entertainment program. During the rest of the time, he led those people to the Lord.

How many other Christians would have volunteered to take part in such a program? No doubt some would have said, "Oh, but I'm a Christian. I don't believe in that sort of entertainment." Not Wigglesworth! He looked on it as a God-given opportunity to share the Gospel with those traveling with him. He was interested, not in the entertainment, but in winning souls for Jesus. He never let an opportunity pass. Nearly every person on the ship knew him as a result of his part in that program, so many doors of opportunity were opened to him for witnessing.

Everything he did in his miraculous ministry was geared toward winning souls for Christ. To Wigglesworth, every sick person healed, every devil-possessed person delivered, every soul saved, every supernatural act was confirmation of the Word of God.

Wigglesworth's priorities were right. Often people say that a person the caliber of Smith Wigglesworth only appears once in a lifetime, as though that is how God purposed it to be. Wigglesworth himself did not agree with this viewpoint. He felt that every true child of God, in his own particular sphere of labor, could be used as much as, if not more than, he was.

The success of Wigglesworth's ministry was not caused by his ability, but rather by his availability. Wigglesworth was available twenty-four hours a day, seven days a week.

God took a nobody named Smith Wigglesworth and used him to shake the world. God used this uneducated plumber, unable to read or write until the age of twenty-six, to confound the learned scholars of theology and to set multitudes free through undisputable signs and wonders. Wigglesworth was used by God in this remarkable way for one simple reason: He made himself available to be used of God.

At the age of eighty-seven, Wigglesworth was still going strong. What is the promise of Psalm 92:12-14?

The righteous shall flourish like the palm tree: he shall grow like a cedar in Lebanon.

Those that be planted in the house of the Lord shall flourish in the courts of our God. They shall bring forth fruit in old age; they shall be fat and flourishing (Heb.: they shall be full of sap).

Wigglesworth was full of sap, full of the life of God.

A Spirit of Faith and Power

Jesus promised His disciples in Acts 1:8:

Ye shall receive power, after that the Holy Ghost is come upon you: and ye shall be witnesses unto me both in Jerusalem, and in all Judea, and in Samaria, and unto the uttermost part of the earth.

The word translated above as *power* in Greek is *dunamis*. From *dunamis* we derive our words *dynamite*, "an explosive force," and *dynamo*, "a power generator." Because the Holy Ghost, the Source of power, is within, *dunamis* comes from within.

Wigglesworth possessed this *dunamis*. He came from the city of Bradford which, to him, was probably the hardest place to minister. Certainly, it was the place which most often saw supernatural manifestations. But also it was the place which showed the least response. As Jesus said, *A prophet is not without honour, save in his own country* (Matt. 13:57).

A man by the name of Mitchell lived not far from Wigglesworth's home. Wigglesworth had talked often with him about his soul, but had little or no response. When he heard that Mitchell had taken ill, Wigglesworth, very concerned about the man's condition, tried to visit him. He knew that unless something was done, the man was going to die. But Mitchell was the hardest case Wigglesworth had ever faced. To compound his concern, Wigglesworth could not get through to see him.

After coming home from an open-air meeting one night, Wigglesworth found that his wife was not home. Learning that she had gone to Mitchell's house, he went also. On arrival, he heard a woman scream. Going up the stairs, he met a distressed Mrs. Mitchell coming down.

"What's up?" he asked.

"My husband is dead."

Wigglesworth entered the room and went to the bed where Mitchell lay. Mrs. Wigglesworth, who was standing beside the bed, said, "Don't Smith. He's dead."

"I couldn't do anything for him while he was alive; he wouldn't believe," replied Wigglesworth. "I can help him now."

"Don't Smith. It's too late," his wife insisted.

All her attempts at persuasion, however, could not alter Wigglesworth's resolve. He prayed, and when he did, life came into that corpse! The man lived for many more years. Who among us would have dared to be so audacious as to attempt such a thing?

Wigglesworth dealt with the situation in the manner he did because he faced it with absolute logic. His family was afraid he might, as they termed it, "overstep the mark," but Wigglesworth said that, as far as God is concerned, there is no difference between his healing a toothache and raising the dead. That is sound logic. People have a tendency toward putting everything-including sin-into categories. But God does not differentiate: Sin is sin, and a miracle is a miracle.

Wigglesworth was practical to the last detail.

To those who did not know him, Smith Wigglesworth seemed unapproachable or untouchable. But this appearance was opposite to what he was really like: loving and kind. Because he always took time to talk to children on their own level, he was greatly loved by them.

When he preached in the poor part of the city where the people were scantily clad, he would go without an overcoat, wanting to feel the cold as they did. He would stand out in the cold street, talking with the people about the Savior.

Wigglesworth never regarded a man's position. He treated the wealthy no differently from the poor, except that he would give the fellow who had to beg for a living some money to buy food.

Wigglesworth was undeterred by opposition or circumstance.

Once in Sweden, crowds of people turned out to listen to him and to bring their sick for prayer. Hundreds were saved and healed. The authorities got the idea that Wigglesworth's motive was to make money, the furthest thing from his mind. For this reason, the police arrested Smith and the pastor of Stockholm's seven-thousand-member Philadelphia Church.

Since no law existed against preaching, they were released. But the authorities warned Wigglesworth not to touch the people to whom he was preaching.

During the meeting he had been preaching to as many as twenty thousand people at one time and praying for the sick individually. He asked God how he should pray now since he was forbidden to lay hands on the people. The Lord led him to pray for them collectively.

He invited all the sick folks to stand and those who could not stand to indicate their need. He told them to put their hands on the affected part of their bodies. Once the people had followed his instructions, he prayed for them. When he did, the power of God swept through that vast company, healing hundreds. Many miracles were outstanding and the authorities could do nothing to prevent them.

A common adage among determined people is, "Where there's a will, there's a way." Wigglesworth's philosophy was, "Where there's a God, there's a way." There is a vast difference between the two.

Once while we were talking in his home about the ministry of healing, Wigglesworth made these observations: "I can see that the ministry of healing is going to get more difficult. It is always more difficult when you have to contend with unbelief. There are already too many remedies in which people put their trust. But I can see that it will get worse, until it will be hard to get people to believe at all. We have become such a drug-conscious society that, in many cases, the aspirin bottle is more important than the anointing bottle.''

Wigglesworth often said, ''I would rather die trusting God than live in unbelief.'' He made this statement not without thought for he came face to face with death more than once. Each time his faith, instead of wavering, only became stronger.

Because he knew how completely devastating unbelief could be, he set himself deliberately to oppose it at all levels. He succeeded. He was never alarmed at any circumstance. The greater the challenge, the greater his resolution was to meet it and win.

His greatest delight in life was to trust God. Jesus said, *And he that sent me is with me: the Father hath not left me alone; for I do always those things that please him* (John 8:29). This last clause is quite a statement. Wigglesworth so loved the Lord that his one consuming passion was to please Him.

Hebrews 11 was Wigglesworth's favorite chapter in the Bible. If any one verse stood out to him in that chapter, it was verse 6: *But without faith it is impossible to please him: for he that cometh to God must believe that he is, and that he is a rewarder of them that diligently seek him.*

Wigglesworth used to say, ''Those people in that chapter triumphed through faith against overwhelming odds—and they were just ordinary folks like me.'' He always looked upon himself as nothing other than ordinary. ''What little I have accomplished for God, anyone who loves the Lord can do, if not more.''

His advent into the ministry was unspectacular. He merely took God at His Word. In return, God took Wigglesworth and used him.

Wigglesworth devoted himself to his ministry. As a result, he became God's man for his day and left his mark upon the world. From the time of the apostles until the present day, few people have made a greater impact upon society than Smith Wigglesworth.

3
Smith Wigglesworth
Life in the Spirit

Because Smith Wigglesworth was so attuned to the Holy Spirit of God, he was keenly aware of satanic activity.

Whether or not it is possible for a person who has been baptized with the Holy Spirit to be possessed by an evil spirit is the topic of endless arguments in Britain today. Wigglesworth claimed that this was possible. He had dealt with such cases and had seen them delivered.

Spiritual Combat

To discern satanic activity, we must live in the presence of Him Who is holy; otherwise, we will very likely fall victim to Satan's wiles. If we maintain the same attitude toward sin and all its by-products that Jesus had, we need never fear the Devil or what he can do. Rather, he will fear us.

Here is an example of this from Wigglesworth's life. During a meeting, Wigglesworth was approaching the pulpit when, suddenly, a man in the congregation started screaming out hideously.

Wigglesworth ran up the aisle toward the man, who got up and ran in the opposite direction. As Wigglesworth tried to get to him, people were knocked off their chairs. When the man reached the end of the row of seats and turned to head for the door, Wigglesworth caught up with him and tackled him. As they fell to the floor, Wigglesworth was shouting, "Come out, you devil, in the name of Jesus!"

Instantly, the man was delivered and accepted the Lord Jesus Christ.

The Holy Spirit had revealed to Wigglesworth that the man was under the influence of an unclean spirit. That spirit had recognized and feared the Holy Spirit in Wigglesworth. Thus the chase.

In confrontation with the powers of darkness, Wigglesworth was never afraid. To my knowledge, he was never defeated when faced with the challenge of a demon-possessed person. Such people were always delivered because the power of the Holy Ghost working through Wigglesworth was so strong.

To discern the seducing spirits which are appearing and multiplying in these last days, we need desperately the help of the Holy Spirit. Wigglesworth, in describing a place he had been, once remarked that the people there were under such satanic delusion that their marriages and homes were breaking up. I wonder what he would think today with so many marriages, even Christian ones, breaking down. Wigglesworth was concerned about this satanic invasion of the sanctity of marriage which he foresaw. His apprehensions were well justified.

According to Wigglesworth, a Holy Ghost-oriented person would not fall victim to the demands of the flesh, regardless of what those demands were. He was persuaded that life in the spirit could so dominate, that the physical body and it's desires could come under the Spirit's control.

Wigglesworth said that a person does not grow old, but grows to maturity. He was full grown. The age or length of time we have been a Christian does not determine our status, but to what extent we are led by God's Spirit. **The evidence of Wigglesworth's development was the he was always led in the right place at the right time in the right circumstance.** Because he was always led by the Spirit, he was always in control.

He used to say, "It is a luxury to be filled with the Spirit. I see everything a failure except that which is done in the Spirit."

Because Wigglesworth was filled with and radiated the Comforter, it was a common experience of both sinner and professing Christian alike to be under great conviction when in Wigglesworth's presence. For the same reason, those of God's people undergoing trials found wonderful consolation in Wigglesworth's presence.

Wigglesworth said, "We should be like torches, purifying the very atmosphere wherever we go, moving back the forces of wickedness."

Once I asked him what he did for relaxation. He said, "I find my relaxation in the presence of the Lord. That is all I need. Any other form of relaxation is not for me, because I am continually doing battle with the Devil. Any form of relaxation apart from being in God's presence would leave me wide open to the adversary."

No wonder he accomplished the great things for God that he did. The forces of darkness held no terrors for him because whenever he met them, he was fresh from the pure atmosphere of the throne room. He carried that purifying atmosphere into the polluted atmosphere of this world, causing devil-possessed people, who recognized him as the servant of the Most High God, to cry out in his presence.

The Sword of the Spirit

Having the authority of the Word of God behind him, Wigglesworth was as bold as a lion. Without the Bible to back us up, we are on a shaky foundation. Nothing breeds fear so much as an unsure foundation. When we demonstrate faith in God's

Word, God will perform His Word, confirming it by signs following: *And they went forth, and preached every where, the Lord working with them, and confirming the word with signs following* (Mark 16:20).

Smith Wigglesworth lived according to the Word of God. As a result, he saw God confirm His Word to such an extent that he was surprised, not when a miracle happened, but when one didn't. Whenever a miracle didn't happen, Wigglesworth wanted to know why, and he was not left in doubt for very long. He shared the same confidence of his God that Abraham enjoyed: *Shall I hide from Abraham that thing which I do?* (Gen. 18:17).

Sometimes we regard the status of the great characters of the Bible as being unattainable, but we should not do so. We need only to have a similar dedication as theirs to be able to enjoy the same confidence in the Almighty they did. In fact, the standard of attainment in God's Word is Christ Himself.

> *And he gave some, apostles; and some, prophets; and some, evangelists; and some, pastors and teachers; for the perfecting of the saints, for the work of the ministry, for the edifying of the body of Christ:*
>
> *Till we all come in the unity of the faith, and of the knowledge of the Son of God, unto a perfect man, unto the measure of the stature of the fulness of Christ.*
>
> *Ephesians 4:11-13*

The Spirit of God does not record such words to mock us but to place a standard there for us to attain. The person who came nearest to attaining that standard of any I have known was Smith Wigglesworth.

Because Wigglesworth's dedication to God was total, he had no worries or fears. God deals with all that is calculated to bring anxiety. His promise means as much as the fulfillment.

Wigglesworth had absolute confidence and trust in the Lord. He loved to sing a refrain which expressed his assurance that God could not fail those who put their trust in Him:

> *He cannot fail, for He is God.*
> *He cannot fail, He's pledged His Word.*
> *He cannot fail, He'll see you through.*
> *He cannot fail, He'll answer you.*

A. E. Mellors, pastor of my home church for twenty-six years and a great Bible teacher, clearly defined faith. In his estimation, faith is comprised of three things:

1. Facts to be believed

2. Commands to be obeyed

3. Promises to be enjoyed

These three points sum up the life and ministry of Smith Wigglesworth, for he believed implicitly the

Word of God. As far as he was concerned, there was no substitute. Believing it, he was totally committed to obeying it. The result was that he enjoyed the promises of God even before their fulfillment.

Wigglesworth would say, "Faith comes by hearing, and hearing by the Word of God, not by reading commentaries. Faith is the principle of the Word of God. The Holy Spirit, Who inspired the Word, is called the Spirit of Truth; and as we receive with meekness the engrafted Word, faith springs up in our hearts."

One day Wigglesworth was traveling by train and seated in a compartment with two women. Talking with them, he soon learned that they were mother and daughter, both sick.

"I have a very reliable remedy in my bag," he told them. "In fact, I have never known it to fail."

He talked so much about this marvelous remedy that the ladies asked him if he would give them a dose of it. In response, he took out his Bible and read to them: *I am the Lord that healeth thee* (Ex. 15:26). It was not very long before God had healed them both.

Once a lady in Cardiff, South Wales, asked him what he would recommend as the best tracts for witnessing. "Matthew, Mark, Luke, and John," he responded, with no further elaboration.

"Folks are always wanting promises to stand on," he used to say. When one young man asked him, "Can you give me a promise to stand on?" Wigglesworth answered by placing his Bible on the ground and saying, "Stand on that."

Hesitantly, the young man stood on it.

Wigglesworth said, "Now you are standing on a great heap of promises. Believe every one of them."

"There are four principles we need to maintain," he used to explain. "Firstly, read the Word of God. Secondly, consume the Word until it consumes you. Thirdly, believe the Word. Fourthly, act on the Word. I never consider myself fully dressed unless I have a copy of the Word of God in my pocket."

While other people might read a book, newspaper, or magazine while traveling, he always read the Word, as he did at every available opportunity. He said, "The Word of God is full, final, reliable, up to date. Our attitude toward it must be one of unquestioned obedience. If a thing is in the Bible, it is so. It is not even to be prayed about. It is to be received and acted upon."

Wigglesworth had the Word of God and the Word of God had him. Just as the Lord Jesus—the Word of God personified—was moved by compassion, Wigglesworth—so dominated by the Word—was also moved by compassion when faced with the needs of humanity.

That compassion, rather than waning through the years, grew in intensity. With this compassion there burned a consuming zeal; and because Wigglesworth lived and moved by the Spirit of God, this zeal appeared on occasion to be aggressive. In the Spirit he was fearless.

In one large crusade, a young woman was among the vast number of people who came forward for prayer. By the Spirit, God revealed to Wigglesworth that this young woman was living a very unchaste life. Not wanting to embarrass her, he spoke quietly to her. "Go home, and sin no more," he said. "God will heal you."

She left the meeting, but came back the next night. At the invitation for those with needs to come forward, she came with the others. Looking straight at her, Wigglesworth spoke out loud and clear, "I told you last night to go and sin no more, and God would heal you. Get out."

Only a person under the anointing of the Holy Spirit could do such a thing without causing absolute havoc. The divine authority with which Wigglesworth spoke had a sobering effect on the congregation.

Notice that the first night he dealt compassionately with the young woman. Had she done what he told her, she would have been healed. By divine revelation, Wigglesworth knew that she had not altered her behavior after she left the meeting. He always knew the mind of the Spirit when he acted as he did.

Smith Wigglesworth was highly criticized. But because he always followed the pattern of God's Word, he always proved his point, though that was never his purpose. His aim, his only goal, was to meet the needs of the people. Because God always vindicated him, he was never embarrassed.

He was equally unmoved by both approval and criticism. He used to say, ''I am not moved by what I see or hear, but I am moved by what I believe.''

The Shield of Faith

Though Wigglesworth did not often spend long seasons in prayer and fasting, he lived an undeniably consistent life of confidence in his God. To Wigglesworth, Jesus' words meant exactly what they said. When Jairus, the ruler of the synagogue, was informed that his daughter was dead, Jesus said, *Only believe* (Mark 5:36).

Down through the years a refrain which contained these words, precious to him, became his theme song. One always heard it in every meeting Wigglesworth conducted. If the congregation didn't sing it, Wigglesworth did.

> *Only believe, only believe.*
> *All things are possible.*
> *Only believe.*

For the next verse, he would change the words to *Lord, I believe.* Often the effects were tremendous:

people being healed and blessed where they stood. Often the whole congregation would be standing by the time the refrain was sung. When the spiritual temperature had risen, Wigglesworth would say, "Anyone can be *ordinary*, but a person filled with the Holy Spirit must be *extraordinary.*"

Speaking on the question, "What is faith?" he would quote Hebrews 11:1,2. *Now faith is the substance of things hoped for, the evidence of things not seen. For by it the elders obtained a good report.* Then he would add, "Men of faith always have a good report."

Another of his favorite quotes was, "Fear looks, faith jumps." He often told his audiences, "I am not here to entertain you, but to bring you to the place where you can laugh at the impossible."

He loved the verse in Luke that says, *For with God nothing shall be impossible* (Luke 1:37). Since he believed this verse, he could never understand why Christians had reservations about it. In his words, "We have got to get rid of our small measure of faith, because God's measure is so much greater than ours. A measure that cannot be measured."

Great fights produce great faith. Wigglesworth enjoyed the greatest season of supernatural ministry during the period of time that he endured the greatest physical affliction. A doctor, whom he knew well, persuaded him to have an X-ray examination. Mainly to find out the extent of his illness, Wigglesworth obliged.

The X ray revealed the presence of kidney stones in an advanced stage. The doctor said there was only one option open: to operate immediately. To this, Wigglesworth responded, "The God Who made this body is the One Who can heal it. No knife shall ever cut it."

"But what about the stones?" the doctor asked.

"God will deal with them."

Shaking his head, the doctor said, "If He ever does, I shall be interested to know about it."

"You shall know."

As the pain increased, Wigglesworth suffered indescribable agony. When ministering on the Isle of Man, he had lost so much blood that his face was pale. From there, he went to Sweden and held a meeting, full of tremendous blessings.

His son-in-law, James Salter, there with him, later told me, "Night after night, Wigglesworth was in and out of bed trying to pass the stones, often rolling on the floor in agony. Yet he never missed a service, and ministered to as many as a thousand sick folks in one day." Even though Wigglesworth was in worse condition than many of those for whom he prayed, tremendous miracles were wrought. When he undressed at night, his underclothing was soaked with blood.

From Sweden he went to Norway. Still the pain continued. Then he went to Switzerland and held a great revival. Multitudes were saved and healed. But Wigglesworth found no relief. Few people knew that he was going through the biggest test of his life. By faith he rose above it.

He went to America and swept through the country like a prairie fire. Thousands were saved and healed during this blessed campaign. By this time, he had been fighting the battle of his life for six long years.

James Salter said, "Sharing his room over those years, I marveled at the unquenched zeal with which he preached and the amazing compassion he manifested in his ministry to the sick. I have seen many people break down under lesser tests than his. He passed hundreds of stones. It was a miracle."

Wigglesworth came through this grueling test with his fire-tried faith stronger than ever, and with a trust in God all hell could not shake. That period of glorious ministry left an unerasable impact upon this world so great that it is still being felt, and will continue to be until Jesus returns.

Wigglesworth's telling me one week before he died that God would take him from the scene was not mere conjecture. He spoke by the Holy Ghost. Fifteen years previously he had said, "I am asking the Lord for fifteen more years of life and service." God granted this request down to the very week.

When he was seventy-two years old, he made that request. During those fifteen extra years of glorious ministry, he preached and ministered throughout Europe, America, and South Africa. He also had a great burden for his native land then, having seen ominous signs. He talked to me about this subject only a week before his death.

"Where is there any faith?" he used to ask. "I can get more out of God by believing Him for one minute than by shouting at Him all night."

He guarded jealously the faith he preached and practiced. On one occasion he said, "Don't you settle for anything less than the best. And there is nothing better than a life of faith: It brings challenge and excitement."

To his listeners, he would say, "Two things will cause you to leap out of yourselves into the great promises of God. One is purity, the other is faith. God has no room for the man who looks back, thinks back, or acts back."

When speaking of Wigglesworth's audacious faith, James Salter often said, "We accompanied him on his great crusades with trepidation, for we never knew what he was going to do next. We were always afraid he would go 'too far.' But he never did. He always said, 'You can't go too far with God; in fact, you can't go far enough.' "

God, bound by His own immutable Word, never let Wigglesworth down. In Mark 11:23,24 Jesus said:

> *For verily I say unto you, That whosoever shall say unto this mountain, Be thou removed, and be thou cast into the sea; and shall not doubt in his heart, but shall believe that those things which he saith shall come to pass; he shall have whatsoever he saith.*

> *Therefore I say unto you, What things soever ye desire, when ye pray, believe that ye receive them, and ye shall have them.*

Smith Wigglesworth lived by and acted upon this principle, and God responded.

We need to demonstrate the same kind of faith, love, and commitment to service which characterized Wigglesworth's life and ministry; but we must never try to mimic him. Whenever we pattern ourselves after any man other than the Lord Jesus Christ, no matter how great that man may be, a potential danger exists.

Spirit-Led Ministry

Never having been attached to any religious body, Wigglesworth's unofficial credentials consisted of the anointing and direction of God's Holy Spirit. With these credentials, Wigglesworth was never in any place very long before the whole area knew him.

He astounded the people who knew him with the zeal he manifested.

From the days of the Bowland Street Mission in Bradford to the last day of his long and fruitful life, Wigglesworth's existence was marked by non-stop ministry. Because of his faithfulness concerning what is sometimes looked upon as mere detail, his ministry was greatly blessed.

Wigglesworth accomplished what he did for God without formal education, yet this simple man of God reached many intellectuals. Because of the anointing upon his ministry, he was mighty. He used to say, "Libraries make swelled heads, but the Word of God makes enlarged hearts."

To Smith Wigglesworth, the anointing of the Holy Spirit was the prime requisite for ministry, the essential motivating and empowering force in every Christian endeavor. He could never understand Christians who could not or would not acknowledge that truth.

Once in Cardiff, South Wales, a man who was genuinely concerned for God's work called a large gathering of Christian leaders. Unity and harmony were among the themes of the conference. But emphasis was also placed upon the need for what Wigglesworth felt were two essentials of ministry: the Holy Spirit and personal holiness.

Fearing that offense might be taken otherwise, the speakers dealt with these subjects in very general terms. The convention was going smoothly, and its organizer was quite satisfied with its undisturbed tone.

Suddenly, Wigglesworth was stirred to the depths of his soul. He thought, *All of these folks are missing God's best. Can I remain criminally silent and not tell the people in this great audience that there is a mighty baptism in the Holy Spirit for every one of them like that which the disciples received on the day of Pentecost?*

Causing no small stir, he took off his coat and mounted the platform to challenge the people. These were his words:

"Friends, if I had all of what you now have *before* I was baptized with the Holy Spirit, then what did I receive in that experience? What do I now have *in addition* to what I had when I possessed what you now do?"

He followed those words with his testimony:

"I was saved in the Methodist Church when I was eight years of age. I was confirmed by the bishop in the Church of England. I was baptized by immersion in the Baptist Church and had the grounding in Bible teaching in the Plymouth Brethren.

"I marched with the Salvation Army, learning to win souls in the open air, and received the blessing of sanctification under the teaching of Reader Harris and the Pentecostal League. I claimed the gift of the Holy Spirit by faith as I waited for ten days before the Lord.

"When I was in Sunderland in 1907, I knelt before God and had an Acts 2:4 experience: I received the Holy Spirit and spoke with new tongues as did that company on the day of Pentecost. That put my experience outside the range of argument, but inside the record of God's Word. God gave me the Holy Spirit as He did to them at the beginning."

He continued: "I want harmony, unity, and oneness, but I want them God's way. In the Acts of the Apostles, speaking with new tongues was the sign of the infilling and outflowing of the Holy Spirit. I do not believe that God has changed His methods."

When Wigglesworth finished speaking, a tense atmosphere filled the place. The chairman hurriedly closed the meeting, but it was too late: Wigglesworth had already laid down the challenge.

Feeling that the importance of the baptism with the Holy Spirit should not be minimized for the sake of religious harmony, he never lowered his standard. Zealously and fearlessly he contended that this experience is invariably accompanied by the speaking with other tongues as the Spirit gives utterance.

Continually, he sounded out the challenge to all Christians:

"Live ready. If you have to get ready when the opportunity comes your way, it will be too late. Opportunity does not wait, not even while you pray. You must not have to get ready, you must live ready at all times."

"Be filled with the Spirit; that is, be soaked with the Spirit. Be so soaked that every thread in the fabric of your life will have received the requisite rue of the Spirit. Then when you are misused and squeezed to the wall, all that will ooze out of you will be the nature of Christ."

O.G. Miles, a pastor and great friend of Wigglesworth's relates a remarkable incident illustrating the leading of the Holy Spirit in Wigglesworth's life.

One day Wigglesworth and James Salter visited Miles at home in Leeds. Suddenly, Wigglesworth said to the two men, "God is telling me to go to Ilkley Moor." He was speaking of a lovely town frequented by tourists about sixteen miles away. Because of the war, gasoline was rationed, but Miles said he would drive them.

When they arrived, they stopped at a lovely spot known as the Cow and Calf Rocks. No soul was in sight, so they seated themselves on an overlook.

For some time, nothing happened, causing Miles and Salter to think that Wigglesworth must have been mistaken. However, Wigglesworth had no misgivings and he was soon proven correct.

A young man with a pack on his back appeared and sat down for a rest next to Wigglesworth. Soon the two were talking. The young man was a backslider who, like the prodigal, was disillusioned with sin. In a few moments there on the moor, the man knelt with Wigglesworth and came back to God.

"What a prayer meeting we had that day on Ilkley Moor!" Miles later said.

Then as suddenly as before, Wigglesworth said, "George, you can take me back now. I have done what God told me to do." How this man was in touch with heaven, waiting for word from the throne for anything God wanted him to do! And the Lord certainly knew who to send on such an important mission: His faithful and trusted friend, Smith Wigglesworth.

Maintaining constant contact with the throne and listening for the voice of God's Holy Spirit was all that mattered to Wigglesworth. Herein lie the secrets of Wigglesworth's success. He could say with Jesus: *My meat is to do the will of him that sent me, and to finish his work* (John 4:34).

Wigglesworth's Power of Impartation

Even though Smith Wigglesworth has gone to his reward for faithful service, he left behind a legacy of his amazing ministry. The Scripture in Hebrews 11:4, which applied to Abel, certainly applied to Wigglesworth.

> *By faith Abel offered unto God a more excellent sacrifice than Cain, by which he obtained witness that he was righteous, God testifying of his gifts; and by it he being dead yet speaketh.*

Since Wigglesworth's death, God certainly testified of his gift in as much that since his homegoing his life has touched the lives of many.

My brother went to see Wigglesworth at his home. And as he was about to take his leave to return home, Wigglesworth laid hands on him and committed him to the work of the supernatural. Wigglesworth prophesied over him and said, "God will confirm what I have done and said before the week is through." My brother left without replying.

Before the end of the week my brother received a phone call from an orthopaedic surgeon asking him to go immediately to the hospital. A member of the church my brother pastored, Mr. Dobson, had sustained a serious injury at his place of work. Both of Mr. Dobson's hands and arms were crushed, yet he refused surgery. My brother went, as the doctor requested, and was asked to explain the seriousness of the injury as the doctor felt he was not getting through to Mr. Dobson who kept telling the doctor that the Lord would heal him. The doctor was most concerned, as gangrene had set in, and he said the situation necessitated an operation to spare Mr. Dobson's life.

My brother prayed for Mr. Dobson with the result being that Mr. Dobson was back at his work in two days! The news went all over the area. A few days later, the day being Sunday, a young lady with her mother, hearing about Mr. Dobson's healing, took the young lady's baby to the evening meeting. The child was totally blind, having been born without eyes. On giving the appeal, my brother asked if there were any who had a need. The young lady and her mother told my brother about the baby's need. My brother closed his eyes and prayed, and as he prayed, he opened his eyes to see the eyes forming in The child's head: The child was healed of a dreadful affliction!

The prophecy of Wigglesworth for my brother had come to pass in the week as said. It was an example of Wigglesworth having the power by the Holy Spirit to impart this amazing ministry to others. My brother from that time on was used mightily of God in the years to come until, at the age of eighty-two, he went to be with the Lord.

Another example of Wigglesworth's ability to impart his supernatural ministry to another occurred when my son was three-and-a-half years of age.

Wigglesworth laid his hands on him committing the young child to the work of the supernatural. Obviously my son was too young to remember this happening, but the evidence was obvious. The blessing of impartation has rested on him, by many being delivered from the power of the devil and many being remarkably healed.

On a visit of my son to Yugoslavia in recent years, a young girl was brought to the meeting where my son was. She had had an eye completely destroyed by a stick being thrust into it; all that could be seen was an ugly white mass. He laid hands on her, and the eye was restored.

Recently, a lady suffering from cancer in a moment was healed. The healing was confirmed by the hospital which diagnosed her case.

I could tell of many sins of people being revealed to my son. Such revelation would fall under the category of the Word of Knowledge, one of the gifts of the Holy Spirit. How necessary a gift this is.

One example that comes to mind is a man in a church well known to me. The man was always ready to do all he could for the church. But it was revealed to my son that this man was taking his wife and three children to the church, leaving them there, then he was picking up a girl, 13 years of age, in his estate car, driving to a park close by, having intercourse with her, then taking her back to the church. This was pointed out to the diaconate who refused to accept the allegation. However, a few weeks later a daily newspaper printed the sordid story exactly as seen by my son through revelation. The newspaper heading read, "Man sentenced to seven years imprisonment for unlawful intercourse with a girl under the age of consent."

Paul writes about imparting spiritual gifts in his epistle to the Romans.

> *For I long to see you, that I may impart unto you some spiritual gift, to the end ye may be established.*
>
> *Romans 1:11*

We can only impart what we have, like Peter and John going to the temple to pray seeing the lame man begging to eke out a meager living. Peter said, *Silver and gold have I none; but such as I have give I thee: In the name of Jesus Christ of Nazareth rise up and walk* (Acts 3:6). Wigglesworth said, when referring to this event, "He was asking for alms but he got legs instead."

Wigglesworth imparted what he had. What a remarkable experience as seen in his laying his hands on a child of such tender years as three and a half, then in later years seeing such a ministry reveal itself: Who can doubt such a ministry!

Wigglesworth was an ordinary working man but with an extraordinary Source of power. Smith

Wigglesworth is gone, but that work remains. Dare we leave it unfinished?

Additional copies of this book
are available from
your local bookstore.

HARRISON HOUSE
Tulsa, OK 74153

Prayer of Salvation

A born-again, committed relationship with God is the key to the victorious life. Jesus, the Son of God laid down His life and rose again so that we could spend eternity with Him in heaven and experience His absolute best on earth. The Bible says, **"For God so loved the world, that he gave his only begotten Son, that whosoever believeth in him should not perish, but have everlasting life"** (John 3:16).

It is the will of God that everyone receive eternal salvation. The way to receive this salvation is to call upon the name of Jesus and confess Him as your Lord. The Bible says, **"That if thou shalt confess with thy mouth the Lord Jesus, and shalt believe in thine heart that God hath raised him from the dead, thou shalt be saved. For whosoever shall call upon the name of the Lord shall be saved"** (Romans 10:9-10,13).

Jesus has given salvation, healing and countless benefits to all who call upon His name. These benefits can be yours if you receive Him into your heart by praying this prayer.

Heavenly Father, I come to You admitting that I am a sinner. Right now, I choose to turn away from sin, and I ask You to cleanse me of all unrighteousness. I believe that Your Son, Jesus died on the cross to take away my sins. I also believe that He rose again from the dead so that I might be justified and made righteous through faith in Him. I call upon the name of Jesus Christ to be the Savior and Lord of my life. Jesus, I choose to follow You, and ask that You fill me with the power of the Holy Spirit. I declare that right now, I am a born-again child of God. I am free from sin, and full of the righteousness of God. I am saved in Jesus' name, Amen.

If you have prayed this prayer to receive Jesus Christ as your Savior, or if this book has changed your life, we would like to hear from you. Please write us at:

Harrison House Publishers
P.O. Box 35035
Tulsa, Oklahoma 74153

You can also visit us on the web at
www.harrisonhouse.com